DOIS I. ROSSER JR. & ELLEN VAUGHN

THE GOD WHO HUNG ON THE CROSS

HOW GOD USES ORDINARY PEOPLE TO BUILD HIS CHURCH

ICM 25*th* Anniversary
Commemorative Edition

Featuring reflections on 25 years
of ministry by Dois Rosser

FOREWORD BY CHUCK COLSON

The God Who Hung on the Cross - *ICM 25th Anniversary Commemorative Edition*
Copyright© 2003, 2011 by International Cooperating Ministries

Requests for information should be addressed to:

International Cooperating Ministries
606 Aberdeen Road
Hampton, Virginia 23661

Library of Congress Cataloging-in-Publication Data

Rosser, Dois I.

    The God Who Hung on the Cross / Dois I. Rosser, Jr. and Ellen Vaughn.
      p. cm.
    Includes bibliographical references.
    ISBN 978-0-9794047-3-3 (hc) 978-0-9794047-4-0 (pbk)
    1. Mission of the church. 2. Church. 3. Christianity — 20th century.
    4. Christianity — United States. 5. Christian life. I. Vaughn, Ellen Santilli.

Printed in the United States of America.

Table of Contents

Reflections by Dois Rosser

Foreword by Chuck Colson

Part 3: The Commission: "As You Are Going"

With Gratitude

Reflections by Dois Rosser

When we originally wrote <u>The God Who Hung on the Cross</u> ten years ago, we had no idea how God would use it . . . but gradually, people all over the world read this little book and became new friends and partners in ministry. They told us how God had used it to deepen their faith in Him. We were amazed.

But perhaps we shouldn't have been surprised by the overwhelming response to this book. Throughout the history of this ministry, God has used small things for His huge purposes. He's showed us, over and over, that nothing happens by accident or coincidence. He links people and opportunities. He gives vision and the means to achieve it. He provides resources, tools, everything needed to advance His Kingdom. He is constantly at work in and through His people.

So it's not by chance that you're reading this 25th anniversary edition of this book. We hope God will use it to refresh and challenge you, and that you'll see in these pages the unmistakable power of God to do far above and beyond whatever we can imagine. For the first 25 years of this ministry, that has been His pattern.

We can't wait to see what He'll do in the next 25 years!

Of course, Dick Woodward and I may not be around for the next quarter century. As I write this, I'm 89 and Dick is 80. But even though we're two old guys, we are finding these days to be among the most exciting of our lives . . . not because of our vigor, of course, but because of what <u>God</u> is doing and what He's allowing us to see in terms of this ministry's outreach and the wonderful fruit of His Spirit in 58 nations.

Even at our ages, Dick and I are still works in process. We're still amazed that God would use people like us for His eternal purposes. When I read the Bible, though, I see that's what He's always done. God calls imperfect people and uses them so it's clear that it's <u>His</u> power at work, not ours.

When this ministry first started, there were really two things that got me going.

The first was Dick Woodward's Mini Bible College. Before I encountered Dick, I had never heard the Bible taught in such a clear, practical, compelling way. I figured that if Dick had developed his teaching so that a character like me could understand the Bible, then we needed to get that teaching out everywhere, so lots of other characters could get it! I wanted to distribute the Mini Bible College to as many people around the world as we could.

The second impetus for me was my work with Billy Graham and the first Lausanne Congress on World Evangelization. I heard Billy Graham, John Stott, and other spiritual giants in Switzerland as they shared what was happening in Africa where God was moving in powerful ways. At the time, World Vision estimated that 16,000 people were coming to faith in Christ every single day on that continent.

But the problem was that many of these new converts didn't have sound, ongoing biblical teaching. The young believers weren't being taught and trained in the strong truths of the Scriptures, and so they were vulnerable to all kinds of false teachings, cults, and instability in their faith. Many withered and fell away from their initial commitment to Christ.

So I was absolutely compelled by the idea that new believers—not just in Africa, but all over the world—needed <u>nurturing</u> in their faith. They needed strong, clear, biblical teaching that could ground and sustain them when the winds of adversity or heresy might blow. They needed real fellowship, accountability, encouragement, community, and they needed to pass on their faith, serving the needs of those around them and introducing their families and neighbors to the reality of Jesus Christ.

In short, they needed the means that Christ Himself established two thousand years ago. They needed His system for flawed human beings to grow in Him and extend His Gospel to others. <u>They needed the Church.</u>

The church is not a building; it is a gathering of people. The building is where you house the assembly. These local assemblies of believers are the way that God changes the world. They are part of what theologians call the "church universal," i.e., the people called by Jesus' name all over this planet. They are the love of Jesus' life.

When He was talking with His disciples just before His crucifixion, Jesus told them, "…whoever believes in me will do the works I have been doing, and they will do even greater things than these, because I am going to the Father." (John 14:12)

How in the world would human beings be able to do even greater things than Christ Himself?

When Jesus was on earth, He was just one person. But after He rose from the dead, ascended to heaven, and gave us the gift of His Holy Spirit, we are now millions and millions of people all over the world—His Church—multiplying His work exponentially.

Really, when He established the church as His way to change the world, He was setting up the ultimate franchising system. Some people don't like it when I call the church a franchise; maybe it sounds too secular. But I think it fits. A franchise is simply the right or license granted to a group to market a company's goods or services in a particular territory.

And as far as I'm concerned, Jesus commissions local churches, almost like franchises, to provide His good news and services to their communities. When churches do that, their areas, then regions, then whole nations will change dramatically.

That's why we're so excited about what God is doing through ICM in places like Tanzania. Tanzania is a country in East Africa with about 40 million people. It's about twice the size of California. Our goal is to build a church every 25 miles, on average, across that country. That's 547 churches, each one committed to plant five daughter churches, so you can imagine how the final result will be a "web" effect across the whole nation, with a church within the walking distance of every Tanzanian woman, man, and child.

As I write, we've built almost 400 churches there. We estimate that we will have blanketed Tanzania with our goal of 547 churches and thousands of daughter congregations within just a few more years.

There are 1.2 billion people in the country of India. Of that figure, many of them are heading to a godless eternity. This is what spurs us forward with great urgency. We have built more than a thousand churches in India . . . and we estimate that we will have blanketed that entire nation within just six or seven more years.

As Billy Graham said many years ago, you can't send enough missionaries to begin to reach a nation of 1.2 billion people. You cannot reach into a nation like India, with its 600,000 villages, unless indigenous peoples are involved, working as "barefoot evangelists." And by the grace of God, there are now thousands of barefoot evangelists reaching out to their neighbors, taking the Word of God deeper and deeper into villages all over India.

God has blessed us with tools that leverage the work of all these indigenous evangelists even more. At ICM, we are committed to use every type of technology possible to get the Word of God into people's heads and hearts. In the beginning, we disseminated the Mini Bible College primarily through radio, which was great. Then as technology advanced, the Internet opened up all kinds of new possibilities.

Right now we're also using hand-held digital technology. These are small, tough, solar-powered audio players loaded with 221 specially-chosen Mini Bible College lessons in the listeners' language. We call these digital units GodPods, and as I write there are 28,000 small group Bible studies using digital players and CDs—and accompanying teachers' guides and student workbooks—to learn about Jesus and deepen their understanding of the Scriptures.

Sometimes people ask us how we measure the effectiveness of ICM's ministry. As you know, we are very careful to leverage every donor dollar . . . and what we look for in terms of results is simple. We look for fruit. The fruit of changed lives, people coming to know Christ, people growing in the mature knowledge of the Word of God and passing His love and truth on to others. And the great thing is this: because of the power of the Holy Spirit, if people are truly nurtured in a local church and truly taking in the Word of God, they will bear fruit. It's inevitable.

So it's fitting for me to open the 25th Anniversary Edition of this book with just a few stories . . . some fresh fruit that God has cultivated through the work of His people all over the world. I hope these few thumbnail sketches will inspire you as they have me!

In India, in the state of Andhra Pradesh on the east coast, one of ICM's very first churches was built in a town called Kotasiralam. A beautiful, unwavering young woman in that church heard the Mini Bible College on the radio; she became determined to get its Gospel message to unreached tribal people.

This tribe, known as the Sora people, lived in remote villages in the hills, wearing loincloths, growing a few crops, and hunting small game with spears and arrows. They intermarried, sometimes practicing polygamy, and looked to shamans to serve as intermediaries between the world of the living and the world of the dead. These shamans would often go into trances, during which the spirits of the dead would speak through them.

Understandably, the Sora people lived in fear, constantly needing to placate deities who were thought to control their crops and rain. There were darker gods to be appeased as well; those who might cause drought or sickness received offerings of animal sacrifices.

The determined young woman in Kotasiralam could not rest with the thought of these tribal people living in fear and bondage. No one had ever made the journey to their villages to tell them about Christ.

Finally a group of Christians from the church agreed to go. They hiked and hacked their way through the jungle for eight hours before they arrived at the first Sora village. They shared the Gospel. Astonished, overwhelmed with the joy of this good news, everyone in the village decided to follow Christ. The delighted barefoot evangelists made their way to the next village, and the next, with similar results. So they eventually built a daughter church in the area.

Three years later, that same church had built 73 daughter churches in Sora areas. Recently we went to visit one of those churches. As we arrived at the village, we were met by a huge group of smiling, exuberant brothers and sisters in Christ—4,000 of them. Through interpreters, they told us, "We represent the 16,000 Sora who have come to Christ!"

And today, when you travel to a Sora village—and I hope you will—you'll be greeted by a delegation armed not with Stone Age weapons, but towels, basins, and water pitchers. They will call you brother, or sister. They will take you by the hand to a seat and ask you to take off your shoes. And then they will wash your feet with cool water, and gently dry them with clean towels.

All because of one determined woman who would not give up on the Gospel going into this primitive area!

Thousands of miles away, in Uzbekistan, the population is more than 90 percent Muslim. We have built five churches there. Obviously this is a tough part of the world to advance the Gospel; we take delight in every church that goes up, knowing that as we lift up Jesus wherever we can, He will draw people to Himself.

There's a phrase we hear a lot in these countries that are so strongly controlled by Muslims: "You can't do that here, but if you want to, you can."

That doesn't make a whole lot of sense, but I love it, because God clearly wants to build churches in Uzbekistan, and so He's doing it.

In a town called Nurabut, there's a church in an area

predominately populated by deaf people. Most of the local population scorns people who cannot hear; in fact, the local term used for them is the same as the word for "garbage."

The pastor and believers in Nurabut knew that God sees people with disabilities quite differently. So they learned sign language and began to connect with the hearing-impaired community, building friendships and letting them know of the overwhelming love of Christ. Gradually the congregation began to grow . . . and now that little church is overflowing with members who will not hear with their ears this side of heaven, but who praise the Lord in unforgettable ways.

During a recent service there, our colleague Burt Reed "heard" a quartet signing hymns, with a sort of reverse translation of a hearing person explaining what the quartet was signing. He took communion with many who were formerly rejected by the society around them as garbage, now welcomed into the family of God.

Burt took a video of the end of the service, with the congregation worshipping God with the hymn, "I Surrender All." Most of the members are signing the words, with a few singing out loud. I have never seen a more poignant rendering of that great hymn; I can't watch that video without weeping with the wonder of what God does.

Thousands of miles away, in Liberia, we work with partners who have weathered terrible storms in their work for Christ. They are leaders of the highest caliber, as you'll see from these two stories.

It's only been about seven years since Liberia's terrible civil war ended. During this tribal conflict, rebels massacred more than 250,000 men, women, and children. Our ICM partner Bishop Jerome Klibo lost his father when a soldier burst into the family home and grabbed his dad, who was 75 years old. As horrified family members screamed and wept, the soldier threatened them all, and then hacked the elderly man to death with a machete.

Years later, Bishop Klibo and the rest of their family were rebuilding their ministry in their ravaged country. Then a visitor arrived in the bishop's office one day. Trembling, terrified, he fell to his knees, then prostrate on the floor. Bishop Klibo knew who he was: the very soldier who had so viciously killed his father.

The man wept on the floor, begging Bishop Klibo for forgiveness. His conscience had condemned him for years, and now he was destitute, broken, desperate for forgiveness, but knowing full well he did not deserve it.

Bishop Klibo thought about all the times God had forgiven him. He thought of Jesus, bleeding on the cross. "I forgive you," he told the cowering man. "I forgive you."

Astonished, the man lifted his head. Bishop Klibo called to his wife to make a meal, invited the former soldier into his home, and broke bread with him. He gave him money so he could start fresh . . . but most important, he passed on the ultimate new beginning of life in Christ.

During Liberia's civil war, another of our ministry partners, Reverend Claudius Deah, found himself in a role he'd never imagined. As the rapacious rebel soldiers sought out fugitives, they'd kill anyone they found on the streets. Rev. Deah began hiding people in his home . . . and before he knew it, some 375 people were crammed into his four-bedroom house, including a number of wounded, elderly, and small children.

The rebel troops were drawing closer and closer to his neighborhood, and Rev. Deah knew he had to lead these people in an escape across the border into Guinea. One night, as gunfire erupted on streets near his home, he and his enormous flock slipped out his back door, one by one, into the darkness, away from the town and into the jungle.

As this modern-day Moses led his people through village after village in the journey to the border, more and more fleeing people joined their exodus. As the huge group approached the border, they ran into armed rebels. The soldiers were perhaps sympathetic; they didn't kill them on the spot, but told Rev. Deah that he and everyone in his group would be killed for sure if they continued their journey.

Rev. Deah would not be stopped. "The battle is the Lord's," he told the soldiers. "He has gone before us. We must press on."

At this, to his astonishment, the weary soldiers laid down their rifles. They had had enough of killing. "We will come with you," they said.

And by the time Rev. Deah reached Guinea, his group of refugees had grown to about 17,000 people. Together, safely, they crossed the border, leaving Liberia behind.

When the war there ended, Rev. Deah established a church-planting ministry, first in Guinea, then Liberia, then five other West African nations. ICM is humbled to work with this modern-day Moses!

In Vietnam, a pastor from Ho Chi Minh City, Thanh Huynh, felt that God was leading him to reach people in Ca Mau, a city in the southern tip of his country. He traveled there, preached, baptized new believers, and rescued street children. For these terrible "crimes," he was arrested repeatedly, harassed, and let go.

One night the policeman who kept arresting Pastor Thanh Huynh took him to the local police station. When the policeman was asked by his superiors to give a report about the pastor's activities, he opened his mouth to respond . . . and found that he was utterly unable to speak. He could not say anything.

So the authorities had to let the pastor go.

Dumbfounded by this experience—literally—the policeman got a report a few weeks later that Pastor Thanh Huynh was back in town. He snuck to the meeting, but this time, instead of just arresting the pastor, he listened. He heard the Gospel. He decided to follow Jesus.

That former policeman went to seminary, and today, he is the pastor of one of the five churches that ICM has built in the Ca Mau area!

In Zanzibar, a beautiful island off the coast of Tanzania, ICM has built 14 churches. One of them is pastored by a man with a very dark past.

Years ago, when he was 28, he was a witch doctor. He performed naked rituals at night, gaining more and more power and becoming well known in his area. But he wanted to become more powerful than his rivals. He had performed all sorts of blood sacrifices, but felt that if he truly wanted more dark power, he needed to make a more dramatic sacrifice.

So he took his two-year-old son, held him up before the spirits, and killed him. More power did come over him . . . powers of bondage, horror, darkness and shame.

Eventually this haunted man heard the only news that could save him. He came to a crusade and heard the Gospel, of the ultimate sacrifice that could cleanse even the most horrible blood guilt. He fell on his face and gave his life to Jesus. He was baptized, began to learn the Bible, and after training, was selected to become a pastor. Today he regularly returns to towns still under the influence of evil spirits, and tells the people about Christ.

In Ethiopia, we've built 32 churches. We were visiting one of them and saw an old shed on the property. "What's that?" we asked.

"That's the 'persecution house,'" our host told us. "Whenever a family in our church comes under persecution, we bring them here to the shed so we can protect them and take care of them." Some members of his church, facing threats and opposition from local Muslims, had lived in the shed for months at a time.

I cannot help but think of our comfortable lives as believers in America, where the need for a "persecution house" is an unknown concept. We have been given so much in terms of monetary blessings and religious freedom! The question is, how are we using what we've been given?

I have learned so much from our friends and partners around the world. These are people who are pouring out their lives in service to Jesus, in the face of persecution, difficulties, natural disasters, afflictions of all kinds. Yet they press on.

I want to do the same as I close in on the finish line of this life. As never before, I feel a sense of urgency as I look at what is happening all around the world. We don't know when Christ will return—but we've got to get His Word out, as much as possible, so that people can come to know Him. These are times when believers need to be either hot or cold, get on board with what God is doing, or go ahead and get off the bus.

Sometimes people will ask me, "How do I finish strong?" I think what they mean is that a lot of us start with great gusto in our spiritual lives, but then peter out over time. I think it just comes down to this: we must have a willingness to step up and *do* whatever God calls us to do . . . we must *implement*, or it remains just a good idea.

So to go back to the two things that got me going 25 years ago, you can see the idea God planted inside my tough old head. First He showed me Dick Woodward's unparalleled teaching on the entire Bible. And then He showed me both the great need for that teaching, and the distribution system that He Himself had established. It was clear to me that all we had to do was to move forward into His will for us to put those elements together and reach into people's villages and communities all over the world.

So we started International Cooperating Ministries as a means toward that end.

Obviously ICM isn't perfect, because it's made up of imperfect people. I'm sure we miss a lot. But I can also say that the nurturing component is at the heart of this ministry, always has been, and that God has led us in a way that our leveraging and return on investment of ministry dollars is truly remarkable. As Dick has always said, get people into God's Word and God's Word into people, because then wonderful and miraculous things happen!

So it's by the power of God that we have a total of 28,000 small groups studying the Bible with MegaVoice and many other means, all around the world. The Mini Bible College is available in 26 languages spoken by four billion people. In 13 different countries, almost 6,000 children who were once abandoned on the street are now growing up in secure, nurturing ICM church-based/orphanages. We've built more than 3,800 churches in 58 nations; these have in turn established an estimated 22,000 daughter congregations. And God alone knows how many millions of lives have been touched and changed for eternity!

All this is happening with a staff that is about the same size that it's been most of these 25 years: *less than 25 people.* That's great leveraging!

And because of God's power, we believe He'll continue to do even greater things than He already has through ICM. So as we've considered the way God has worked in the past, we've set some bold vision goals for the future. In the next nine years, by the end of 2020 we've prayerfully resolved to:

- have built or under construction 10,000 churches;
- facilitated 100,000 small-group Bible studies;
- and discipled one million evangelists around the world.

Those are daring goals. There's no way a small team of people working away in a little headquarters building in Hampton, Virginia can make that happen.

Impossible.

But this isn't about us. It's all about God, and the way He works through His chosen delivery system, churches all over this world. So I think as you read this book and enjoy its amazing and wonderful stories, you'll see, yet again, that with God, <u>nothing</u> is impossible!

Dois Rosser
Hampton, Virginia
March 29, 2011

Foreword

Chuck Colson

I met Dois Rosser soon after I became a Christian. I was at the National Prayer Breakfast, and my host, Doug Coe, seated me next to Dois. I soon realized why. Dois is committed to Christ and overflows with His compassion. Dois never judges people— not even a notorious Nixon hatchet man who was so hated in those Watergate days. Dois became a brother right then and there.

As I got to know Dois better, my respect for him grew. His lively, lovely family was a testimony to his relationship with his wife, Shirley, and their consistent Christian parenting. In some ways he was different from me; he seemed gentle and easygoing, with a Southerner's courtly manner. But I realized that under Dois's laid-back exterior was a sharp, relentless mind that didn't miss much, and he had an urgent determination to maximize his time on this earth for the Kingdom of God.

Once Dois heard a conversation between me and another man during a retreat at a Young Life camp in North Carolina. We were talking about investing in the film *Born Again*. Dois never said a word. Typical. He just looks and listens and soaks up information. Later, he quietly came over to me and said that if we needed it, he'd like to put $150,000 into the movie. We did, and he did–and that money was largely lost. Though the film was an evangelistic success, it was a financial bust. But over the years, Dois has never even mentioned it. He's the kind of friend everyone dreams of having.

As I grew in the faith, and Prison Fellowship grew as well, I realized that this was the kind of solid, deeply committed, sacrificial, bighearted man that I would like to come alongside me and be part of the building up of the ministry. With great trepidation, I asked him if he would be interested in serving on our Board of Directors. I knew he received many such requests, and our Board doesn't do anything in terms of remuneration or recognition or perks, unless you count going into prisons a bonus. It's a hardworking Board that takes responsibility for Prison Fellowship's ministry and holds it to tough standards of excellence and accountability.

To my surprise and delight, Dois agreed, and he has been one of my stalwart counselors for more than twenty years. I've been able to trust him totally, tell him anything, and know that he would keep my confidences utterly. I knew too that if he challenged or probed me, it was because he had my best interest in mind as a brother in Christ. He has never had an agenda of his own. His motivation has always been to do whatever he could to better serve Christ and help his brothers and sisters in the Lord.

As the years went by, Dois and Shirley and Patty and I spent a lot of time together. But I have to admit that I had Dois pegged primarily as a businessman who had given his money, time, and expertise generously to Prison Fellowship and many other ministries.

Little did I realize that he had a heart like the apostle Paul and a similar ability to endure tough travel to places that were *way* off the beaten track. Little did I dream that this wealthy suburban entrepreneur would find his greatest fulfillment in fellowship with believers in mud huts in the wilds of India, Africa and other needy places.

So Dois started International Cooperating Ministries. At first I thought he was dabbling, but it was soon clear that Dois had put his business expertise to work, designing a powerful and strategic church-planting initiative. At a time in life when most of his peers were relaxing, playing golf, and spending their days at the country club, Dois was off eating strange food in stranger places and building up the Body of Christ around the world.

This book is an adventure story, because that's what *really* following Christ is—the greatest adventure of all. Dois lives that to the fullest!

There are so many lessons we can draw from Dois's life. The first is the biggest. He evidences the truth of the challenge given to Dwight L. Moody: "The world has yet to see what God can do through one man fully committed to Him." As you know, Dwight Moody prayed that he might be such a man—and he went on to evangelize two continents for Christ.

Dois is a person wholly committed to Christ. He's not perfect, but long after he has passed on, people of many, many tribes and nations from the four corners of this earth will be worshiping the living God—because of Dois's vision, perseverance, generosity, commitment, and sacrifice.

Dois also shows us that it is never too late in life to take on something big for God. He was at retirement age when he started International Cooperating Ministries. He not only gives me the encouragement to think big, but to do small things with great love as well. We need not wait for huge, cosmic solutions to the needs in our world today. If we do, we'll never do anything. The fact is, we can't love the whole world at once. But we can love individuals and communities of people as God gives opportunities—if we are insightful and courageous enough to take those opportunities. That's what Dois is doing, and in this book you'll see the remarkable fruits that have come from his quiet obedience.

As you read, you'll enjoy the journey. That's because this book was cowritten with my beloved friend and colleague, Ellen

Vaughn. Ellen, who has collaborated with me on nine books, writes absolutely beautiful prose. In some ways, this book is a sequel to our book, *The Body*, for it vividly illustrates the reality of how Christ is building His Church, His Body, around the world.

This is the remarkable story of the difference one person, fully committed to Christ, can make. May God use it to spur you on to make a difference in your own part of the world today!

Charles W. Colson

Part 1: The Call: Out of the Box!

An Unexpected Story
Ellen

Sometimes you come across a great, life-changing story when you least expect it.

The story that follows in this book began when I was sitting at my desk one day, minding my own business. The phone rang. It was a man named Dois Rosser. He asked if I was available to help him write a book.

Because I had worked with Chuck Colson for many years, I knew Dois as one of Chuck's closest friends, a member of Prison Fellowship's board of directors. An amiable Southern gentleman and successful entrepreneur, he had made a good deal of money in car dealerships, real estate development, and other businesses. I had even bought a used car from this man. So you could say I knew Dois.

What I didn't know was that he is a *radical* brother in Christ, someone to whom God speaks in unusual ways. I didn't know he had taken his earthly fortune and invested it in the work of building churches around the world, from Vietnam and Nepal to Cuba and Zimbabwe. I didn't know he was broadcasting the Gospel via radio and Internet around the world, including many nations whose governments are hostile to Christianity.

Nor did I know that Dois had an incredible story to tell. It isn't really about what *Dois* is doing, but what *God* is doing.

You won't see these stories on CNN or read about them in your newspaper, but Jesus Christ is building His church in some of the most unlikely places around the world today. He's using all kinds of people to do so.

About ten days after Dois called me, I found myself in the jungles of Southeast Asia, traveling with him by helicopter, airplane, oxcart, moped, water buffalo, and river barge in Cambodia, Vietnam, and China. (Did I mention that Dois is in his eighties?)

Later I journeyed with him to strange places in India, Ukraine, Cuba, and the Amazon jungle. I wanted to go with Dois to meet with believers in the African bush and the deserts of Mongolia, but he drawled, "Honey, those trips are just too tough." So he went without me.

As I walked with Dois–or rather, ran with Dois—on his *easier* trips, I saw some secrets of the faith that compel this brother. I saw stories that God is writing for eternity in the lives of people around the world. I felt a new urgency to pursue God's surprising quests, however I could.

What follows is not just an armchair travelogue. As I've run with Dois and seen how God works through him, some key principles have emerged–truths that can transform those who have grown weary on the journey, and tools that can equip us in these crucial times, *wherever* we live.

I believe God most often works through paradox. So it is fitting, I think, that this story of hope and transformation begins in one of the most utterly hopeless places on earth.

The Killing Fields
Ellen

The Vietnam War churned for years, destroying lives in Southeast Asia, dividing America, shaping generations to come.

But by the spring of 1975, the end was beginning. Communist forces were closing in from the north, and there was panic in the streets of Saigon. Overloaded American helicopters hovered over the U.S. Embassy, staggering with their cargo of sweating Americans and terrified South Vietnamese. Few would ever forget the sight of those they left behind. Thousands of men and women had stormed the embassy compound, many clinging—briefly—to the choppers' landing gear, desperate in their doomed attempt to escape.

As the American helicopters roared out of Vietnam, communist forces were taking power in neighboring Cambodia.

Led by the brutal revolutionary Pol Pot, the Khmer Rouge entered the capital city of Phnom Penh, their signature red scarves tied around their necks and fluttering from the barrels of their rifles. They marched the city's two million citizens into the countryside, and Phnom Penh became a ghost town remade in the barbaric image of Pol Pot's philosophy. His soldiers burned books and destroyed medical equipment, hospitals, communications, highways—every vestige of western technology and every element of the country's infrastructure.

Only the radios were left untouched, so that Pol Pot's party–
Angka Loeu, or "Organization on High"–might communicate
his will to the masses.

But the greatest destruction was reserved for the people
themselves, as all the "undesirable" societal elements on Pol Pot's
list were obliterated.

The list was long–doctors, monks, journalists, those who
spoke French, those who wore eyeglasses, those too young or
too old to work for the party on High. As many as three million human beings–a third of the country's population–were
beheaded, shot, bludgeoned, drowned, strangled, buried alive,
or slowly tortured to death.

Their bodies rotted in mass graves, but their battered skulls
endured to become the chief symbols of Pol Pot's mad regime.
Those who lived were sent to the labor and reeducation camps,
where anyone aged five and older was expected to work sixteen
hours a day. Those who could not meet production quotas
were killed on the spot. Schooling and family structures were
obliterated. Children were rewarded for allegiance to Pol Pot–or
"Uncle"–and educated only in the fine art of informing on their
parents.

Millions suffered and died.

In 1979, when Vietnamese forces invaded Cambodia, Pol
Pot and his Khmer Rouge were forced to flee into the jungle. He
was sentenced to death in absentia on charges of genocide and
finally died under detention by his own troops in 1998.

By the turn of the millennium, the kingdom of Cambodia,
ruled by Prime Minister Hun Sen, was still a place of disorder,
political corruption, and random violence. Its countryside was
still studded with millions of landmines, its cities filled with children orphaned by AIDS. The average citizen's life expectancy
was forty-seven years of age.

While neighboring countries gained new prosperity,
Cambodia's per capita income remained at about $180 a year.

The sole business that flourished was its brothel system, particularly its traffic in child prostitution.

It seemed to be a land without hope.

Fields of Harvest
Ellen

I peered from the open porthole as the big helicopter flew over the flooded rice paddies of Cambodia, curious about what this war-torn land would look like so many years after the conflict in Southeast Asia. The heaviest rains in twenty years had immersed the countryside in a tide of muddy water. The rainy season was past, but the dirt roads below us, bumpy at the best of times, were now impassable bogs of rutted mud.

But Dois Rosser is not a person to get stuck in the mud. Ever entrepreneurial, he had somehow managed to rent this mammoth, Soviet-era helicopter–and now, here we were, skimming above the treetops, the old engine roaring in our ears. We were on our way to see the churches and orphanages that Dois and his friends had built in this ruined land.

It had already been a long journey. I had left Washington on a Monday to connect with Dois and seventeen other travelers. We logged the miles from the East Coast to Dallas to Seoul to Hong Kong to Phnom Penh, crossing the International Date Line somewhere along the way and losing Tuesday forever. I wondered if I would be a day younger when I died. As the trip went on, I wondered if it would happen soon.

When we arrived in Phnom Penh late Wednesday, we were sweaty and exhausted. Dois's partner in Cambodia, Ted Olbrich, met us at the airport. He handed out water bottles, cautioned us to keep up our fluid intake in the extreme heat, and took us straight to the site of Cambodia's Tuol Sleng Museum, a grisly monument to Cambodians who were tortured, imprisoned, and killed by the Khmer Rouge. The murderous things we saw there were overwhelming.

A few hours later we arrived at our hotel. The corners of the building were peaked and pronged; that traditional Asian architecture, we were told, was designed to keep evil spirits from entering the building.

I wasn't sure it worked. The corridors were dark. Frayed, live electrical cords ran up the walls; small green lizards ran down. Monkeys shrieked in the trees outside. It seemed ever so slightly haunted.

Exhausted, we slept for a few hours. The lizards skittered up and down the walls. The travel alarm went off at 4:45 A.M. At 5:30 our weary group left for the military airport, ready to take our journey into the jungle.

At the air base our van drove directly onto the cracked tarmac. An ancient Soviet helicopter sat about twenty-five yards away. Its rotors were bent like the antennae of a damaged insect. Its fuselage was worn. Its three tires were flat.

Oh, I thought. *I guess part of the airport is set aside as a museum for antique aircraft. How nice.*

Then our guide motioned us toward the monstrosity. I began to realize this was to be our transportation for the next two days. We climbed up a rickety pull-down ladder. Inside the rusted shell the seams didn't quite meet. Looking toward the aft wall I could see blue sky through the cracks in the fuselage.

Sixteen red plastic lawn chairs provided seating for most of our group; evidently when this helicopter was constructed, seat belts hadn't quite yet been invented. A big, bright yellow gas tank was screwed to the long wall next to the open oval doorway. "No smoking" signs and other dire warnings in Russian hung on the pitted walls above it. Frankly, smoking was just not something that had occurred to me.

I have never been a great flyer. Even in state-of-the-art aircraft, it is all too easy for me to vividly envision my own death. Once I panicked just a teeny little bit and tore the armrest off a plane seat during some turbulence on a flight to New York.

But now, in this helicopter in Cambodia, it was not a case of irrational panic. This was pure, cold logic at work. As I looked at this contraption and its pilots—one of whom was sitting on an upended box—I knew we were going to die. And so did most of my fellow travelers.

"Let's pray," someone said. We did. Then, as one of the crew members heaved the rusty hatch shut, we took our places on the plastic lawn chairs.

The ancient engines roared to life. The propellers spun. The yellow fuel tank jiggled. Committed, my companions and I just looked at each other and grinned wildly. The helicopter shuddered, shook, and then pitched forward like a nauseated person running for the restroom.

Then, against every known principle of physics, it lifted vertically into the air, sputtered a few times, and there we were, skimming above the treetops.

The jungle air rushed past the portholes. Realizing I was still alive, I was filled with an absolute wave of exhilaration. I laughed out loud like a crazy person and put my face as near the open porthole as I could without my contacts blowing out of my eyes.

Below, narrow boats, like peapods, navigated the pools that had been rice paddies before the floods. Farmers poled through the shallow waters, inspecting the ruined plants that had once been their crops. I could see Buddhist temples in the distance; miles of green; swift flocks of trim white birds, their shadows following them across the surface of the muddy water.

Suddenly Ted Olbrich shouted over the roar of the engines. "There it is!"

I looked into the distance, and there was the slender steeple of a church rising above the green treetops, its wooden cross silhouetted against the sky.

The helicopter circled. Now I could see a man waving a long stick with scarlet fabric tied to one end. The arcs of the bright flag marked our landing place, a muddy patch of ground between two flooded gulches.

"That's Pastor Heng Gkum Hi!" Ted shouted.

We all looked at him, not quite sure if he had said something or sneezed. "Bless you!" someone shouted back.

The helicopter settled slowly, the wind from its propellers flattening the jungle trees and banana plants. We touched down. The rotors slowly stopped.

In the sudden silence I could hear the giggling of dozens of children, and then, the sound of singing.

"Welcome! Welcome!" called the pastor. He and two elders bowed, their palms pressed together in the traditional Cambodian greeting. They grasped our hands. "Come!"

We followed them down a muddy path. Then we saw the church, its white walls shimmering in the tropical heat, and standing in front of it in a long line were dozens and dozens of small children, singing, smiling, and laughing as they saw our sweaty group stumble from the jungle.

"This is the day!" they sang in English, carefully following their pastor's wife, who served as choirmaster. "This is the day that the Lord has made! Let us rejoice and be glad in it!"

We looked at the fresh faces, so eager and full of hope. A small girl with dark eyes and deep dimples smiled and bowed to me. Then she came forward and grabbed my hand, and we walked together to the church that is also her home.

That little girl is still in my mind. I don't even know her name. But God does; her joyful face is a perfect picture of the awesome yet personal power of God at work. In the places of need, despair, and desolation, He brings comfort, hope, and power.

How did Christ's hope come to those children in rural Cambodia? How were their lives rescued from starvation, cruelty, AIDS, prostitution, and other perils?

The short answer is that Dois' work, in partnership with several other ministries, built that orphanage (and many others like it). It's not just an orphanage, but a church as well. The congregation meets on the first floor, and the children live in dorms on the second. These simple facilities cost about $30,000 in American dollars to build.

Each church-orphanage houses twenty-five to fifty children who would otherwise live as prey on the streets. Instead, they now receive food, education, some medical care, and the Gospel. They believe in God because they have seen His love in a smile, a hug, a bowl of rice, and a safe place to sleep.

They know the security and support of His people because they are growing up in stable church homes; they're being discipled in the truths of the Scriptures, and they're learning music, computer science, and vocational skills as well.

As they grow up with these advantages, these children may well become the leaders who can pilot their unstable nation toward a new era of hope.

Dois and his International Cooperating Ministries team have built more than 100 church-orphanages in Cambodia, which have planted over 2,000 daughter congregations. These provide sanctuary for more than 5,000 children and sanctuaries for about 20,000 Cambodian adults.

But new hope in Cambodia–or anywhere else–begins not with one particular ministry, but with God, and the odd truth that He chooses to do miracles through ordinary people as they are willing to be used by Him.

That's why this book is not just about Dois Rosser. It's about how God can use each of us, right where we are–as long as we are willing to break out of the boxes that bind us.

Most of us gravitate toward boxes. It's human nature. We seek what is comfortable and familiar. Sometimes we are loath to leave the litter in our boxes even to make positive changes because we don't want to move beyond the parameters of what we've always done.

But Jesus is not one for boxes. He broke out of the tomb that held Him. He freed His friend Lazarus too. He threw the money lenders' boxes right out of the Temple. In His earthly ministry, He constantly pierced people's puffy conventions and challenged their earthly comforts, luring them toward the risky business of eternal comfort. He challenged the rich young ruler to give up the wealth that defined and confined him. He wooed the woman at the well to be free of the sin that bound her.

And, in one of the passages I love most, He called His disciples to "put out into deep water." In Luke 5, we're told that Christ's friends had been in the shallows, and that's where they wanted to stay.

"Come," Jesus said.

Grumbling, they rowed to where the water was deep, and the lake was wide. They were in over their heads. Jesus rocked their boats.

And then the shimmering fish leapt into the nets, the men strained to haul the catch, and Peter fell at Jesus' feet, overwhelmed by the power of the living God.

In our own journeys with Jesus, is not the dynamic the same? He calls us further than we would choose to go on our own.

I thought of that after I survived that crazy helicopter trip in Cambodia. Think of it as metaphor: that old Russian helicopter just did not fit my paradigm of safe air travel. It did not conform to the acceptable parameters of what I was willing to trust. But if I had stuck with what was familiar and stayed on solid ground, I would have missed the adventure that followed.

That's what Jesus does! He woos us constantly to come farther in and farther up, to dive deeper into the river of His grace.

Sometimes we resist. We like comfort and the illusion of being in control. But if we stick with what is familiar, we box our faith. It becomes human enterprise rather than godly exercise.

But if we take even the smallest step of willingness–"Oh, Lord, I know not what lies ahead. I can't control it. But I trust You!"–we break out of the box.

Then God takes us on new adventures we could never have imagined.

"What Do You See?"
Ellen

We spent only three days in Cambodia, traveling from village to village. We visited five church-orphanages and met hundreds of children whose lives have been saved. We were showered with songs, scarves, and jasmine blossoms. I watched Dois scramble up and down handmade ladders and bamboo scaffolding, inspecting the buildings that were under construction. He got less sleep than any of us, ate hazardous local food with gusto, carried toddlers on his shoulders, sipped from fresh-cut coconuts, and prayed with Cambodian pastors, draping his long arms around their shoulders as they hugged his waist. He was like a modern-day apostle Paul.

But the apostle Paul did not have a helicopter.

At one stop, after we had flattened the foliage and landed in a pasture amply dotted with water buffalo manure, a party from the church welcomed us. The distance to their building was too far to walk, they said, but they had arranged transportation. They pointed toward the edge of the field, where six wooden carts stood, attached to six bony water buffalo. Our taxis.

We picked our way across the field and climbed into the tumbrels. The buffalo regarded us with derision, then lurched into service. The carts' big wooden wheels slung fat gobs of red mud into the air and onto our clothes.

As we pitched and wobbled down the pitted lane toward the church, villagers scrambled from the grass huts on either side, hiding their faces and pointing their fingers at the Americans. They were laughing too. We felt honored that our mere appearance could bring such joy to an entire village.

But no matter how we arrived at each church-orphanage, the story was the same: Lives changed now and for eternity.

As we stood at each site, Dois would put his hand on my shoulder. *"Ellen, what do you see?"* he would ask.

I saw a young boy, maybe nine, with freshly healing wounds on his belly. He had been working in the field with his parents a few months earlier. The plow had hit a land mine that had lain buried for thirty years. In a moment, the mother and father had been torn apart, and the boy had taken shrapnel in his stomach. Now he and his four brothers were orphans.

I saw a little girl with cross earrings in her pierced ears. We didn't speak the same language, but when I pointed to them and then to the cross I wore around my own neck, she pointed up to the sky. We'll see each other in heaven.

I saw one of the women in our group pull a plastic jump rope from her huge purse. She handed an end to one of the orphans. The two turned the bright rope. Little clouds of pink dust rose where the rope smacked the ground. The children hung back, shy for a moment, but then two small boys ran for the rope and jumped into the middle, their dark hair flying as they leapt and laughed.

I saw men and women from the village who were not yet part of the church. Some of their children were naked, their hair matted, their legs bruised and covered with scabs. They watched us curiously and listened as the Cambodian pastor preached about the love of Jesus.

"What do you see?"

"I was hungry and you gave me something to eat, I was thirsty and you gave me something to drink, I was a stranger and you invited me in, I needed clothes and you clothed me, I was sick and you looked after me, I was in prison and you came to visit me."

["When did we do that for You?" ask the faithful.]

"Ah," replies the King,] "I tell you the truth, whatever you did for one of the least of these brothers of mine, you did for me" (Matt. 25:35-36, 40).

At home where we are comfortable, those well-known words can seem distant. But when we visit with people who are hungry, thirsty, strangers, naked, sick, and in prison, Matthew 25 becomes more than a memory verse. It speaks to the strange, supernatural reality of actually serving Jesus–a reality we can miss when we stay in our boxes and neglect to go out to people in need.

So in the wilds of Cambodia I saw Jesus. Sometimes He was in a distressing disguise, as Mother Teresa used to say about her service to the sick and dying in Calcutta. But I saw Him in those who were so needy, and I also saw Him in His people, gathered together to worship Him and to make His love known to others.

In Cambodia, I heard as well. I heard a story that reminded me–again–that I dare not box Christ into my own little expectations of what He will or will not do. It's the story of the God who hung on the cross.

The God Who
Hung on the Cross
Ellen

In September 1999, a pastor we'll call Tuy Seng traveled to
Khampong Tom Province in the north of Cambodia. Pastor
Seng had wanted to bring the Gospel to the remote villages there
for years, but they had been under the control of an isolated
pocket of Khmer Rouge radicals until early 1999.

Now, as far as anyone knew, he was the first person to speak
of Jesus in that isolated area. Most villagers cast their lot with
Buddhism or ancestor worship. Christianity was unheard of.

But when Seng arrived at one small, rural village, the people
welcomed him eagerly. They could not hear enough about the
Gospel. Most made decisions to commit their lives to Christ.
Smiling, Pastor Seng asked the people why it seemed as if they
had been waiting for him to come.

An old woman shuffled to the front of the group, bowed,
and grasped Pastor Seng's hands. "We *have* been waiting," she
said. "We have been waiting for you for twenty years." And then
she told him this story.

After the Khmer Rouge took over Cambodia, they made their
way through the countryside, destroying just about anything created with purpose and design—bridges, highways,   hospitals,
human beings. It took a while, but after they had dealt with
Phnom Penh and other city centers, they focused on the villages.

So it was that the soldiers came to this hamlet in 1979. Their technique was the same as it has been for countless communities, but for the people who lived there the terror was new. The communists emerged from the jungle and strode from hut to hut, ordering the villagers out. Those who resisted were killed at once; many died in front of their homes.

The rest were marched to a clearing behind the village. Their own farm tools were thrust into their hands.

"Now dig!" the soldiers shouted.

The villagers hacked the red-clay soil, trembling with the dark realization that they were digging their own mass grave. Some lost their nerve and tried to run. They were shot and dragged to the edge of the still shallow pit.

Hours passed as the people sweated and wept and dug—until finally the hole was deep enough. The people laid down their spades and shovels. The soldiers shouted for them to turn and face the pit.

They braced themselves, waiting for the killing blows, knowing that the soldiers would bludgeon them to death rather than shoot them—why waste precious bullets on ordinary peasants?

The heavy, humid air lay still as the villagers began to cry out—the wail before death, when the heart's longing to live becomes a desperate plea for help. Some screamed to Buddha, to ancestors, or to demon spirits. A few cried for their mothers.

Then one woman began to cry, intuitively, to one of her earliest memories—the faint echo of a story told her by her mother about the God who hung on the cross. She called out to that God. Surely the One who had suffered Himself might have compassion on those about to die. Time stopped. The humid jungle air lay still.

Suddenly the screams around her became one great wail, as the entire village called out as one, crying for their lives to the God who hung on the cross.

There was only silence.

They sobbed into the darkness of the pit before them.

Silence. A flicker of hope.

And then the people turned, one by one by one.

The jungle was empty. The soldiers were gone.

And ever since that astounding day in 1979, the people of that village had been waiting—waiting for someone to come and tell them more—more about the God who hung on the cross.

Paradox
Ellen

The story of the God who hung on the cross may sound strange to American ears. But it reminds us that Christianity is not about our boxed notions of just who God is and just how He acts. It is about life in the jungle and the threat of death at any time. It is about miraculous intervention and divine rescue.

Perhaps it's hard for American Christians to conceive of a place where people waited for twenty years to hear the Gospel. Many of us drive past half a dozen churches to get to our own. Christian teaching is on the radio and television. We have religious books and newsletters and magazines. We can buy Bibles of every color, targeted to every marketing group.

But in a stark culture like Cambodia's, the severe realities of Christianity's incredible paradoxes stand out all the more clearly.

God became a man.

He took on our weakness, sorrows, and shame.

He died.

Then He burst out of death. He lives.

Today He still works through paradox. He demonstrates His power through weak people and in unlikely places. Like a pagan village in Cambodia.

If you're like me, you think, well, maybe things like that happen. We hear lots of missionary stories. We believe God can intervene in miraculous ways in remote places and deliver people from suffering or injustice or death.

And maybe we prefer it that way. God saves faraway people's lives, on His own. The soldiers slink away into the jungle. The villagers weep with joy and live. When I hear such stories, I don't have to do anything but wonder and worship and try to write them up as best I can.

But the longer I'm on the journey with Jesus, the more it seems that God most often chooses to work in a far more improbable way—He uses *us* to intervene; flawed human beings who don't know what we're doing. He places a person in need in our path, and He gives *us* a choice.

Take Christ's own story of the Good Samaritan. Muggers beat and robbed a man traveling on a dangerous road. We don't know the victim's identity. He was just "a man." Everyman. A priest came down the road. There was the naked, bloody human being right in his path. He had a choice. He decided to cross the street and keep going. Another religious leader did the same.

Then there came the Samaritan, low man in the social pecking order of his day. Same opportunity, different choice. It cost him time, money, and he probably got blood on his robes—but he took care of the person in need.

"Who was the neighbor?" Jesus asks the crowd around Him.

"The one who had mercy," says the lawyer, who like many of us seems to have been an authority in right answers but short on action.

"Go and do likewise," says Jesus.

Now why didn't God intervene and send angels to help that beaten, bloody man? Better yet, why didn't He just prevent the victim's suffering in the first place?

We don't know. It seems that Christ wasn't clarifying all the mysteries of His divine will in that story. It seems He was more interested in making a simpler point: when someone is in need, we must get involved.

It doesn't seem to matter who the needy person is. In fact, the key detail Christ highlighted was that the victim was someone of a different cultural background than the person who helped him. Whatever the case, Jesus did not conveniently limit our responsibility. Barring God miraculously taking care of the situation from above, all we know is that we must stoop and help whomever we find in our path. It takes action on our part.

To change to a metaphor that I don't believe is in the Bible, think of a football stadium. Most of us prefer the scene to look like this: Jesus is the star player, carrying the ball down the field on His way to a touchdown. Single-handedly.

Meanwhile we're pulling for Him from the sidelines. Maybe we're on the bench, confident and clean in our handsome uniforms, drinking Gatorade and staying cool. Or maybe we're cheerleaders, turning handsprings, leading the crowd in the wave, yelling encouragement, and wildly waving our pompoms.

But no. Jesus calls us out on the field. We're in the huddle, but we're not even sure we heard the play. The stadium is packed, and it sounds as though most of the crowd is against us. The field is muddy and slippery. The defensive players are hulking, mean, and absolutely enormous.

There we are, ninety-eight pounds wringing wet. And then Jesus laterals the ball to us. To us! Doesn't He want to win this thing?

Well, yes, He does. And He will. And in His divine perversity, He likes to work this way. Until the final whistle, He is looking to us to carry the ball and play as a team, and we are cheerfully assured that we'll get muddy and beat up in the process.

When we take the ball, or make the choice to help the person in need, we don't know what will happen. To put it in biblical terms, we walk by faith, not by sight.

Think of the quest in Tolkien's *Lord of the Rings* books. Ordinary creatures are up against armies of foul, unspeakable evil. The future of their world is at stake. To prevail, the forces of good must carry the great ring of power and destroy it in the fire in which it was forged. The characters entrusted with this enormous task are not armor-clad knights on swift horses or wizards imbued with vast powers. They are hobbits, less than four feet tall, fond of food and the fireside, the most unlikely means by which the dark might of the ring will be conquered.

In one of the bleakest moments near the end of the story, hobbits Frodo and Sam have traveled far beyond their comfortable, boxy homes. They are weak, filthy, and haven't combed their furry feet in months. Knowing they are not adequate for the huge task they've been given, they are doomed to probable failure—and not likely to forget it since they are headed for a place called Mount Doom. There's little hope. But they know they must go on.

"Our path is laid," says Frodo.

Sam agrees. "We shouldn't be here at all, if we'd known more about it before we started. But I suppose it's often that way."

Sam goes on to talk about adventures. He had assumed great heroes somehow knew how their tale would turn out, and the knowledge of that ending kept them going. Now he understands that heroes are ordinary people who have no clue but just press on, one furry foot in front of the other, until their part is done.

Tolkien's story is not an allegory. Tolkien cordially disliked allegory. But he believed that human stories can reflect the noble truths of God's divine story.

Take Abraham. History reveres him as a great patriarch, but at the time he was called out on strange journeys for which he had no map, he was hobbitlike. "By faith Abraham, when called to go to a place he would later receive as his inheritance, obeyed and went, even though he did not know where he was going" (Heb. 11:8). He walked by faith, not sight.

God gives us great quests every day. We don't usually call them quests—that sounds so grand. We call them opportunities. Sometimes they seem like interruptions.

Some seem manageable, like helping a child in our neighborhood. Others, we know, are absolutely impossible, like rescuing orphans from the brothels of Cambodia. Sometimes God may intervene miraculously and take care of those in need with a flick of the faintest edges of His huge power. But more often He gives such tasks to us. He places people in our path, and it is up to us to help them. He puts opportunities before us. It is up to us to pick them up, even though we can't see how the story will end.

Like those orphans in Cambodia: Dois will tell in a later chapter how their needs came to his attention. Many of us might have just passed on by. Dois stopped, picked up the opportunity that was on the path in front of him, considered it carefully, and chose to help. As a result, incredibly, God has saved hundreds and thousands of lives.

Years ago Dois was in Boucha, Ukraine, a suburb of Kiev. Working with an energetic, sausage-consuming pastor named Victor Kulbich, Dois was building churches all over Ukraine. At Victor's church one day, Dois saw a teenaged girl in the distance. A scarf draped her face and shoulders. As she got closer, Victor gently asked her to remove her scarf so Dois could see. Dois's heart twisted. Where Maryna had skin, it was inflamed and contorted. Her gums and teeth were exposed. Parts of her face were missing altogether.

When Maryna was a young child, she had reached up on a stove where her mother was cooking. She tipped a pan of scalding oil, and it cascaded down on her upturned face. It burned off her nose, her ears, and her lips. Much of her skin melted.

Her horrified parents did all they could, but their income was less than $250 a year. The Ukrainian doctors patched Maryna, and the toddler survived, but as she grew, there were times she wished she had died.

Dois has three daughters. He thought of what it would be like if it had been Janice or Cindy or Pam who had been so horribly burned. He told Pastor Victor that he would do whatever he could.

Dois might have crossed the street and kept on going. As awful as Maryna's suffering was, how could he help? He wasn't a plastic surgeon. His was not a medical ministry. He was already doing good things. Surely somebody else could do something for this girl.

But when Dois got home, he started calling people. He made arrangements for Maryna and her sister, Sasha, to fly to the United States. Then he called a Christian physician, Glenn Sheppard, who said he would perform Maryna's plastic surgeries for free if Dois could find a free operating room—not something you come across every day.

But when we get moving, God gives little miracles along the way. Dois phoned his son-in-law, who had been on the board at a Virginia hospital. Within minutes Gary called him back: "You'll be given, free of charge, the use of the operating room at Mary Immaculate Hospital!"

"God is at work! The Body of Christ is at work!" sputtered Dois after he hung up the phone.

End of story? Not yet. Glenn Sheppard retired, and insurance issues meant he couldn't keep working with Maryna. Dois kept poking around and turned up Dr. N. Ray Lee, who knew of a prominent plastic surgeon in Boston, Julian Pribaz, who agreed to help and donated his services. Another surgeon, Denton Weiss, did follow-up—also for free.

Maryna has had dozens of surgeries, with more to come. But she has new skin, a new face, brand-new hope. She and her sister have lived with Christian families in Virginia. They've taken on baby-sitting and other jobs so they can send money to their parents in Ukraine. And they have been baptized and are part of a local church.

"We love the stories about Jesus healing people in the New Testament," Dois says. "And He still does miracles. But I think most often He heals today through people in the Body using the resources they already have to help people who can't help themselves."

Once Dois was meeting with a bunch of Christians in Santa Clara, Cuba. One of the Cuban women was a leader of great vision and energy. Her dark eyes danced as she talked about how people were so open to the Gospel, how the numbers of believers were growing steadily. She went to a tiny closet and pulled out an enormous map, which showed the downtown area, with a cross marking the spot of their church. Then she pointed to crosses spreading out from that site, a dozen strategic neighborhoods where that mother church had planted, or was targeting to plant, new churches.

An American traveling with Dois described what happened next: "This Cuban woman is talking real fast in Spanish about all that God has done so far and what they believe He's going to do in their town. The translator can barely keep up. I see Dois getting more and more excited. He's got this look in his eyes like Rooster Cogburn–he's ready for action.

"'Are those daughter churches funded?' Dois asks the lady.

"'Some are,' she tells him. But most of them don't have the money to get started, and so she's been waiting to get them going until they have some kind of support.

"Dois is up on his tiptoes, staring at that map like he's gonna buy the whole city for God. 'I'll take 'em!' he says."

Today, those churches are growing and reproducing. As God's Spirit moves like a fresh breeze across Cuba, there are now churches all over that island nation. After decades of official atheism and local spiritism, people are hungry for the Gospel in unprecedented ways.

There are lots of books that tell what has already been done, but don't show what God could do. Our goal in this book is to show what God is already doing so marvelously in some pretty exotic places around the world, and then to build a bridge to where we live. We want to stir up fresh possibilities of what He could well do right here at home.

In the process, I'll highlight Dois and his ministry of partnering with believers in other countries to help them build churches like those churches in Cuba, or those church-orphanages in Cambodia. Dois is not particularly comfortable being in the spotlight. He prefers to operate behind the scenes. But friends have convinced him to share his stories so the rest of us can learn from them. Dois's main hope is that God would be glorified and His Kingdom extended.

Though Dois is still a young man in his eighties, I know he is thinking about a time after he is gone. He wants to leave a reproducible legacy for those who follow. This is his story, and I'm the writer who has helped him tell it. At the beginning of each chapter you've already noticed our names appearing in small type, indicating which one of us is speaking. In the chapters marked with Dois's name I'll sometimes serve as emcee, inserting comments and highlights when Dois prefers not to be in the spotlight. You'll also notice occasional small stories at the ends of chapters; these pick up a theme from overseas and show how it can change lives at home.

Here's how the stories from afar got started.

In 1988 Dois founded a non-profit organization called International Cooperating Ministries. Working with Christian leaders in developing nations, Dois and his team provide congregations money to build churches. As a condition, the people agree to plant five daughter churches. They also agree to contribute a portion of their offerings to a covenant fund, from which those daughter churches can later borrow to construct their own buildings. Then they, in turn, plant more churches. And more. For example, in India six churches started in partnership with ICM established more than 1,700 daughter congregations–in just ten years. Not bad.

Meanwhile Dois and the ICM team produce radio programs and CDs that are distributed in developing nations, some of which are officially closed to the Gospel. These feature the Bible teaching of a pastor named Dick Woodward, and they reach a potential audience of three billion people around the world every day.

As you read this, churches are being built in 47 nations such as Congo, Haiti, and Nepal. They are taking hold and multiplying in Vietnam, China, and Brazil. People can hear the Gospel in their own language in places like Egypt, Iraq, and Saudi Arabia.

Clearly, God is doing something unusual through this little ministry many Christians have never even heard of. Perhaps it's because He loves paradox. He takes a courtly, silver-haired man in his retirement years and has him dangling out of helicopters, helping hopeless orphans, more alive than most twenty-year-olds.

God loves to use people who are too old, too young, too small, too weak. He loves to use little things to effect big changes.

Like this. There's a remote, dusty village in India. A few years ago the men there drank too much and beat their wives. The children wore nothing, and many died young. The women worshiped the trees and carved wooden gods.

Then here comes a crippled Indian guy in a battered wheelchair. He's become a Christian. He has an old radio. He brings the radio to the marketplace each morning, and a small crowd gathers to hear Pastor Dick Woodward talk about Jesus in their language, Telegu. One by one, two by two, people decide the Truth is true. They put their trust in Christ. They throw the household gods into the village cesspool where they belong. They quit bowing to the trees. They send a letter to the address they hear on the radio, and soon a parcel of Bibles arrives. Eventually a young seminarian starts visiting them each Sunday. Their little group grows. Soon a hundred people are gathering each week, until now they're tithing rice and bananas and a little bit of money so their new pastor can eat.

Then they borrow money from Dois' ministry and build a church. Their church plants more churches.

Now that pagan village is mostly Christian. There is a small medical clinic. Alcohol abuse has stopped. Children and adults have learned to read. People take care of their little huts, and their church, freshly painted bright white and blue, flowers planted around it, sits right in the center of the life of their community.

Transformation

God's great paradox is that nations are not changed from the top down but from the bottom up, not by government edicts or kingly proclamations, but by ordinary people's lives being transformed, one by one by one. That was the case in the days of the early church, which eventually rocked the Roman Empire, and it's the case today in places like India.

Dois and his ministry partners are on to something. God can use any of us to make a significant difference for Christ in this broken world. And the means of doing it are not some grand plan or program, but something right there on the path, like an ordinary-looking rock on the trail in front of us. At first we might not recognize it. It may not look like much. Then we might see it as a quest or an opportunity. We might be tempted to dismiss it as an interruption. God gives us the choice: we can choose to pass it by. Or we can pick it up.

HOI!

Dois

To introduce myself, I must tell you I'm a member of HOI.

HOI was founded by Dr. Lloyd Ogilvie, former chaplain of the United States Senate. When Dr. Ogilvie walked the marble hallways of the U.S. Capitol, he would greet dignitaries in his deep, resonant voice. But every once in a while he'd see a senator who was part of his small prayer group. Then Dr. Ogilvie would wave his arm wildly and shout with gusto, "HOI!"

And the distinguished senator from wherever would grin broadly and shout back, "HOI!"

HOI?

Their greeting was that of a not-so-secret society of Christians on Capitol Hill. In spite of their positions of power they were quite aware of their own spiritual powerlessness and their need for a Savior. They were part of HOI–the Holy Order of the Inadequate.

Although I'm no senator, I'm a member of HOI too. I've seen how God works through me–in spite of me. I like the way the apostle Paul put it: "We do not preach ourselves, but Jesus Christ as Lord, and ourselves as your servants for Jesus' sake…. But we have this treasure in jars of clay to show that this all-surpassing power is from God and not from us" (2 Cor. 4:5, 7).

I didn't have a dramatic conversion like many of my friends. That would surely make a better story.

But I've resisted the temptation to invent a wild tale. For whether our stories are exciting or not, God gives each of us a walk through life. Along the way He uses us, and He equips us for the pleasure of spending eternity with Him. We can't understand it, but we have been a part of who He is from the beginning of time, and He can make any life a journey, or a quest, of meaning and adventure.

A Virginia Gentleman

I was born in 1921 in the foothills of Virginia's Blue Ridge Mountains. I was the third of five children. Our home life was built around our church life. As Baptists in the Bible Belt, we didn't dance, smoke, play cards, or drink alcohol. When my dad received gift bottles of liquor at Christmas, he would thank the giver politely–then later he'd call all the kids to the kitchen and make us watch while he poured the Scotch down the sink. Seventy-five years later, I can still smell the fresh pine scent of the Christmas tree along with those fragrant fifths of Johnny Walker Red sliding down the kitchen drain.

As the years went by, my "churchianity" became a real relationship with God. I received Christ in 1933 at the invitation of a preacher in a little country church near Richmond. She presented the Gospel and invited any who wished to receive Christ to come forward. I did.

My dad was my chief role model. He loved people. He was comfortable and outgoing with people of high rank or low. He was an engineer at the Newport News Shipbuilding yard. He was also a gifted gardener. Though he would later grow prize-winning roses as a hobby, back then he grew vegetables for our dinner table. The cow tied in the back yard furnished our family's milk delivery.

We were poor, but I didn't realize it. Dad made $35 a week, which was standard for most people we knew. It was also standard for us to tithe a portion of everything we had to the Lord's work. That was as much a habit as saying grace before every meal, for we understood that everything we had was a gift from God. We were to thank Him for it and manage it wisely, and we were to give to others as we had been blessed.

I graduated from high school in 1939 and went to work in the shipyard. I went to business college at night, worked my way up in the company, and somewhere along the way bought a bright red Ford convertible.

That car was key. One day while driving it, I saw a friend from high school, Shirley Sutton. Shirley was a popular cheerleader, whom I had always admired, but she was way out of my league. She had never really given me a second look–until the day I pulled up next to her in that red sports car. Her eyebrows popped up. When I offered her a ride and she got in, I made a mental note right then and there to go into the car business. Shirley and I were married in the summer of 1943.

I went into the Air Force and served as an auditor while I also played on the Air Force baseball team. After World War II, I spent a few more years in accounting and management, and then God set me out on a career that would equip me for the ministry He had in mind for me–even though I didn't realize it at the time.

Wealth of Opportunities

A partner and I started an insurance and real estate company, which became quite successful. We sold both commercial and residential properties. In 1947 we listed a car business. I wasn't driving that red convertible any longer, but I still thought it would be neat to have a car dealership. So I purchased it with a friend.

I kept one hand in real estate, developing a number of townhouse, single-family homes, and upscale communities. Meanwhile, my partner and I learned as we went along in the car business, did pretty well, bought more dealerships, and developed the POMOCO [Peace Of Mind, Of Course] Auto Group.

God gave Shirley and me three daughters. Pam came to us via adoption, Cindy and Janice the old-fashioned way. Over the years I didn't get a whole lot of time in the bathroom, but I handled being the only male in the household fairly well–except on Sunday mornings when I'd sit in the driveway, honking the horn, while the girls ran around getting ready for church. Late again.

During those years I'd leave home at five o'clock in the morning and come back at seven in the evening for dinner. It was hard on Shirley, but I cut out everything else that might take me away from the family. I dropped out of service clubs, stopped playing golf, and made sure that we took family vacations. All these years later, when we ask the girls their favorite memories, they talk about our family camping trips. Never mind exotic beaches or Europe or the Grand Canyon. They remember us all squeezed together like sardines in our sleeping bags, huddling together while rain splattered the roof of our leaky tent.

As the girls got older, I got back into community clubs, service organizations, and ministries. I served on the boards of directors for Trans World Radio, Leighton Ford Ministries, and Prison Fellowship. I chaired Billy Graham's evangelistic events when Billy would come to the Tidewater area.

God also connected me with Abraham Vereide, Doug Coe, and the Fellowship Foundation in Washington, D.C. We and many others built relationships with men and women on Capitol Hill, in the White House, in diplomatic circles, in business–and as a result, many leaders in positions of influence heard the Gospel. I focused on Virginia, networking with Doug to start small groups, prayer breakfasts, and other ways men and women in my home state could come to know Christ.

Opportunities of Wealth

God blessed us. I was selected for honors in the car industry, which put me into arenas of influence where I was able to watch and learn from some of the key business leaders in America. I bought out my partner, and eventually Shirley and I found ourselves with material wealth far beyond what I had dreamed of back when I was a kid with a paper route.

Although we always tithed and gave generously to our church and Christian ministries, down deep I always sensed a nagging guilt that if I was really serious about Christianity, I'd be in full-time ministry. It was as though I had drawn a dividing line. On one side were "sacred" things: Christian ministry, church activities, missionary outreach. On the other were secular endeavors like car sales, real estate, and my other business dealings.

Well, that was a false division, as I would soon realize.

But first I had to meet a man named Dick Woodward.

A Medium-Sized Giant

Dick was the pastor of the Virginia Beach Chapel, a half-hour drive from our home in Hampton. And during the late 1970s, every Thursday morning at six-thirty, 350 men would assemble in the restaurant of the local baseball stadium to listen to Dick teach from the Bible.

That kind of thing was unheard of in our area. Sure, it was the Bible Belt—everyone went to church on Sundays—but people were calling this breakfast "the Thursday morning happening." Men from all over the area were scrambling to hear Dick Woodward teach them how to apply the Bible to their daily lives.

I was curious, so I went.

When I first saw Dick, I couldn't see why the man had such a following. He was an unpretentious, medium-sized man with medium-brown hair, medium-brown eyes, and a medium-range voice.

Nothing in his outward appearance warned me that God was going to use Dick to turn my life upside down, propel me around the world, give away most of my money, and change my thinking forever.

And that was just for starters.

Fellows in a Ship
Dois

When I went to the prayer breakfast and heard Dick Woodward speak, I was hooked. I had read the Bible for years, had heard it taught since childhood, but I had never heard anything like Dick's teaching. He unpacked the Scriptures phrase by phrase. He was funny and blunt. He spoke in street language. He offered good ideas for practical applications.

Dick didn't notice me at the prayer breakfast. In that baseball-themed restaurant, called the Diamond Club, Dick stood at home plate when he spoke. Among the hundreds of men who were there, I was way off in left field. Appropriate. But eventually I called Dick for lunch, and our friendship began to grow.

Because of my involvement in the Fellowship Foundation, I often recommended speakers for retreats and conferences. So I started recommending Dick. For all of them. He provided a strong alternative to the "Christianity Lite" teaching that is so common—all foam and no body.

Dick and I became a traveling road show. He spoke to gatherings up and down the East Coast. My job was to carry his bags and provide moral support.

As Dick, his wife, Ginny, and Shirley and I spent a lot of time together in the early 1980s, our friendship deepened.

Shirley and Ginny had a lot in common–they are both incredibly lovely women with absolutely no flaws of any kind.

Dick and I, however, had just a few flaws, and we were different in both personality and experience. But God wove our lives together–Dick, a pastor, a gentle spirit, and me, a hard-edged businessman.

Well, Row!

At that time I was meeting with a group of guys every week. We asked Dick to join us. We would take turns leading a devotional thought from the Scriptures, and then we'd tie our discussion to what was happening in each other's lives. If anyone seemed particularly troubled, we would set aside our schedule and hone in on him, even if he didn't want us to.

The idea was to get beneath the surface and challenge each other–just the kinds of relational behaviors that don't come naturally to entrepreneurial, self-sufficient businessmen. Our next nine years together could provide enough material for a book of its own, but most of it would be unprintable. As God grew us together, we learned that real strength doesn't come from individual invulnerability but from corporate vulnerability.

> **Ellen**
>
> *Years ago Dick Woodward started meeting with a man who was new to Christianity and facing overwhelming problems. "There's a word you'll be learning soon," Dick told him. "It's fellowship. It means 'two fellows in the same ship.' I want you to know that I'm in the ship with you, Charlie."*
>
> *The other man looked at Dick, scowled, and blew smoke in his face before he spoke: "Well, I'm ready, let's row, [blank] it!"*

The Legal Pad

Not long after Dick joined our group, I sat down at my kitchen table one morning with a yellow legal pad. After draining a big cup of coffee, I prayed that God would help me get out of my "business as usual" thinking.

It was what writer Bob Buford calls a "half-time" moment. As Bob says, I knew what I believed, but now I needed to plan what I was going to *do* with what I believed. Most people have these half-time considerations at midlife, in their forties. I guess I was a slow learner–I was fifty-nine when I stopped long enough to sit down at the kitchen table and take stock.

I had achieved many successes in the first half of the game, so to speak, but I needed to reevaluate. What was really important? How could I use my time, money, and abilities for things that would, in fact, last *forever?*

I drew a vertical line down the middle of the page. On one side I wrote the heading "Kingdom Business," and on the other, for lack of a better term, I wrote the title "Secular Business." (Shirley suggested I call that side "Monkey Business.") I began to list all the ways I was investing my time and money and other resources, splitting things into one side or the other with my usual division between the holy and the material.

All for One

Suddenly, as if Someone had hit me on the head with a velvet hammer, I sensed God saying, "Dois, don't you realize that they are one and the same?"

God was reminding me of what I should have known all along: there is no divide between Kingdom business and world business, no red margin-line split between the sacred and the secular. It is *all* under His dominion.

He had called me to be a businessman and had equipped me to use my expertise for eternal purposes. I had always assumed that I would make enough money in the business world so I could switch over to Kingdom work later and become a missionary. Now I realized that I was a missionary–a minister of the Gospel–already.

That morning, sitting there with my yellow legal pad, was a watershed. God shook my life to its foundations and led me to something He had specifically planned and designed for me to do.

Then God led my old friend Dick through the most severe shakeup of all.

The Unthinkable

It began slowly. One time Dick and I were with a group of about three hundred men. Since Dick had been having trouble with muscle spasms in his legs, he sat on a stool to teach. After he had finished, the men responded with a standing ovation. As Dick rose to thank them, his legs gave out and he crashed to the floor. Dick being Dick, he laughed it off as we helped him up.

Another time, as Dick was jogging, he was overtaken by an odd sensation, as if his legs just would not obey the commands his brain was sending. He did what most busy people do when their bodies don't cooperate with their schedule's demands. He ignored it. As the weeks went by, he continued to preach and teach and counsel, serving the Lord, bearing fruit, and proving to be seemingly indispensable to the church and community. We prayed for him fervently. Surely God would not remove one of His able warriors from the thick of the field of battle!

Would He?

As we soon discovered, our understanding of the scope of the battlefield and our comprehension of God's paradoxical Kingdom power were very limited.

As the odd episodes continued, Ginny, Dick's family, and the rest of us finally convinced him to go to the doctor—to the Mayo Clinic, in fact, where the medical team kept him for three weeks and evaluated him for every conceivable problem.

The diagnosis came back. Multiple sclerosis.

Years later, we found out that was not correct. Other doctors would discern that Dick had a rare degenerative disease of the spinal cord, though the effect was the same either way.

As time went on, our friend weakened before our eyes. Even before those of us who loved Dick could accept the fact he could not walk, he was losing the strength in his arms as well. The years went by. The disease kept at him. And in the end, our dynamic, colorful, irrepressible friend was laid out like a pale wax image of his former self, immobile in a narrow steel bed.

Today Dick is a quadriplegic. Machines and tubing do his body's work. Though he cannot move he endures terrible, constant pain. He's been stripped of every physical ability that many of us take for granted. His prognosis is not very good.

But the wit and humor are stronger than ever. His fine mind is far more agile than most, and if you spend about five minutes with Dick, you realize that in spite of his physical disability he is full of peace. He overflows with God's ability to bring joy and grace to any circumstance.

Even as God was allowing Dick's physical abilities to deteriorate, He was designing a far more aggressive opportunity to spread his teaching.

Thinking the Unthinkable

In the early 1980s, as Dick's disability began to take him down, we felt a great urgency to preserve his teaching. So while he was still able, we started the process of audio- and videotaping Dick's survey of the entire Bible. He had used it for years in church settings, for training lay people in the Scriptures, even as a regular guest on a television talk show. Dick called his approach the Mini Bible College.

Many great expository teachings of the Scriptures exist, but what makes Dick's teaching unique is its "bottom shelf" quality—it is accessible to anyone. As the radio Bible teacher Alistair Begg says in his Scottish brogue, "With regard to the Bible, the plain things are the main things, and the main things are the plain things."

Since Dick feels as though people's lives really change when they understand and apply God's Word, he teaches the plain things of Scripture in a way that engages both the biblically sophisticated and the theologically illiterate.

With my legendary business savvy, I thought it would cost about $25,000 and take about six months to produce the tapes.

Well, two and a half years–and $100,000–later, the job was done.

But now we had a tremendous tool for spreading the Good News and for discipling new believers. We broadcast the Mini Bible College on local television for two years. Since radio was much cheaper than TV, however, we realized that for the same financial investment we could reach millions, rather than thousands, of people. Also, since people in our Bible-Belt area had lots of ways to hear the Gospel, we thought it would be more strategic to make Dick's teaching available to people with few other spiritual resources.

As a board member of Trans World Radio, I had some relationships and a little bit of knowledge in the broadcasting field. In the beginning, it made sense to broadcast in our own hemispheric backyard. We knew that the small Caribbean island of Bonaire had a major broadcasting tower. It seemed a good launching pad. From Bonaire, Dick's Bible teaching could reach millions in Latin America.

We had no idea, though, how those millions would multiply.

Rethinking the Unthinkable

It was awful to watch disease take Dick down. Between his fortieth and fiftieth birthdays, he went from being a robust, unstoppable man to a quadriplegic, abruptly blocked in the middle of the game.

Dick's ministry of Bible teaching seemed like it would stop too. Then we thought about tapes and television and radio–tools to spread Dick's teaching far further than when confined to his physical presence. Media could multiply the message–and what had been an obstacle became an opportunity. The roadblock of Dick's paralysis became a series of stepping stones that led us higher and higher beyond the limitations of Dick's ministry in our part of Virginia. That was as far as we could see. But God's vision went much further. He had a plan to take Dick's Bible teaching to the whole world.

Maybe you're facing a roadblock right now. I hope it is not as terrible as paralysis. But maybe there's an obstacle that has stopped you in your tracks. The way God does things, that obstacle could actually be an *opportunity* for something much bigger than you could have dreamed. So let me give you a challenge–or far better, let *Dick* give you a challenge.

I Can't–But He Can

Ellen

Whether you're at the top of your game or down for the count, you can probably relate to Dick. He's been a successful mega-pastor, rubbing shoulders with the power brokers of this world; he's also encountered dismal failures. He's been so energetic that he couldn't wait for the alarm clock to go off in the morning– and he's been physically immobilized to the point where he can't even scratch his own nose, let alone leap   anywhere.

But the extremes of Dick's life illustrate the key point. It doesn't matter whether we are strong or weak. It doesn't matter who we are or what we think we can or cannot do. What matters is *who God is–and what He can do*. Once we grasp that, we can enjoy *His* power, regardless of the state we happen to be in.

"I have learned to be content whatever the circumstances. I know what it is to be in need, and I know what it is to have plenty. I have learned the secret of being content in any and every situation, whether well fed or hungry, whether living in plenty or in want. I can do everything through him who gives me strength" (Phil. 4:11-13).

From Zero to Hero

Dick grew up in the middle of a herd of eleven children in Pittsburgh. His devout mom died when he was fourteen. His dad loved God and loved his kids, but he was busy all the time, working as a mail carrier by day and driving a taxi at night. Dick skipped school, hurled rotten tomatoes at passing cars, and got in scrapes with the police.

Dick was a little inept with machines and vehicles. Once, on a job, he drove a truck into a river. He jumped out just in time, but he and nine of his buddies got fired. Later he got a job driving a milk truck but couldn't manage the clutch, which was also the brake if you pushed it down further than halfway. The truck shook and shuddered, glass bottles shattered, and there was spilled milk all over the street.

Dick didn't cry over it, though. It was just another incident in a string of episodes that curdled his self-image.

"I was a zero," he says, "with the circle rubbed out. I had a terrible inferiority complex. Later, when I majored in psychology, I discovered there was nothing complex about my situation at all. I was just plain inferior!"

Then, when Dick was eighteen, his brother-in-law challenged him to give his life to Christ. As a Christian, Dick still drove vehicles off the road—but now he did so with a new sense of purpose.

Eventually he enrolled at Biola University, where he met the first of two powerful mentors. Renowned Bible expositor Dr. J. Vernon McGee was Dick's professor of Old Testament. McGee made Scripture come alive. Dick wanted to make the Word accessible for the masses in the same way McGee was making it accessible to him, so Dick began to think, down deep, about how to preach the whole Word—to the whole world.

But it would take years for that dream to mature.

In 1953, when Dick was twenty-two, McGee came to his dorm room one night. The other students wondered what the great professor wanted with the hapless Woodward.

McGee, who was teaching an eight-week series in another city, asked Dick to drive him. By the end of the eight weeks, their hours in the car together brought Dick a new depth in his understanding, and answers to the questions liberal theology was raising at the time regarding the divine inspiration of the Word.

After graduation, Dick worked as a youth pastor for his second mentor, Ray Stedman, a minister who had just started what would become a large, influential congregation, the Peninsula Bible Church of Palo Alto. Stedman took Dick on as the first of seven hundred young men he would mentor over the years. He had Dick teach thirteen different Bible studies each week—on thirteen different books of the Bible. He met with him for four hours every Thursday afternoon. He loved Dick, and through him, Dick learned to love the Bible.

At that point Dick was still so shy he could barely function around other people. The feedback he received was not always encouraging. Dick had a low-key, casual voice, quite different from many of the fiery orators of the time. "Your content is really great," a parishioner told Dick, "but about your voice... can't you find a good Baptist minister to preach your sermons for you?" (Years later, that calm, conversational tone was the very attribute that made Dick so popular on secular television and radio. His obstacle became an opportunity.)

Dick went on to Dallas Seminary. After his marriage to Ginny Johnson in 1956, he was asked to pastor a small group of people who wanted to start a church in Virginia Beach. Dick led the church for twenty-three years.

The Dismal Decade
In the first six years they grew to a fellowship of about two hundred people and then plateaued, with no new growth for the next seven years. Pastors are supposed to attract new people, build new buildings, and report huge growth. But it wasn't happening. Dick felt like a failure.

On the last day of 1968, Dick was on his way to visit a church member in the hospital when he heard a radio commentator speculate about what the New Year would bring: "Nineteen-sixty-nine looks like more of the same," he said. "More of the same in Indo-China, more of the same in Europe, more of the same all over the world."

Those words chilled Dick's heart, and he nearly crashed yet another car. "Oh, no!" he cried out to God. "Anything but that! If You give me another year like the last one, I'll quit!"

That night Dick was busy preparing a New Year's Eve communion service when God called a particular verse to his attention. It was Jeremiah 33:3: "Ask me and I will tell you some remarkable secrets about what is going to happen here" *(Living Bible)*.

Those fresh words gave Dick a sense of hope. He desperately wanted something new to happen in his church, something remarkable to break into his numbing routine. *A "remarkable secret,"* he thought to himself. *Maybe it will be a call to a big church… or speaking opportunities in new venues….*

What happened to Dick in 1969?

Dick's wife, Ginny, had to be hospitalized repeatedly for crippling, undiagnosed illnesses. At the time, the Woodwards had five young children: two in diapers, and three toddlers.

Dick had never been particularly domestic. Since Ginny had always managed the home front, Dick had absolutely no idea how dirty diapers made the journey from the rank stew of the diaper pail to the drawer of the changing table, all fluffy, clean, and white. (Pampers had not yet been invented.)

Now Dick learned the intricacies of soaking, washing, drying, folding, safety pins, and rubber pants. Ginny, doubled over in pain, could only watch and wonder from afar. The women of the church pitched in with meals, and somehow, everyone survived.

After eleven months of domestic duties and church challenges, after trying harder and harder and getting behinder and behinder, Dick came to the end of his rope one Saturday night.

He was in the midst of a double diaper change. The phone rang. Dick held his daughter down with an elbow, cradled the phone to his shoulder, and continued wiping and pinning.

The person on the other end said she was in crisis, but as Dick listened, he realized she didn't really want help. She just wanted to talk. And talk. Not only was Dick completely unprepared for his sermon the next morning, but his children were screaming, and this person—in spite of the howling in the Woodward home—seemed as if she would talk all night.

Right then, Dick hit the wall.

After managing to hang up, he finished the diaper change, crumpled to the floor of the nursery, and began sobbing uncontrollably.

"I thought this was going to be a 'remarkable' new year," he cried. "This is not what I had in mind!" All his frustrations and fears came tumbling out in a rush. He sobbed out his fears, his failures, his feelings of inadequacy in his ministry.

"God!" he cried out in desperation. "I can't! *I can't!*"

And there, in a heap on the dusty floor of that little nursery, Dick felt God speak.

I've been waiting thirteen years to hear you say that, he seemed to hear God say. *Now let's see if you can learn this: I can!*

That diaper epiphany changed Dick's life. He realized it was okay to be inadequate. Inadequate people, in fact, are the only people God has to work with: "God, who said, 'Let light shine out of darkness,' made his light shine in our hearts to give us the light of the knowledge of the glory of God in the face of Christ. But we have this treasure in jars of clay to show that this all-surpassing power is from God and not from us" (2 Cor. 4:6-7).

Most of us know the truth of that verse intellectually. But often, like the pre-epiphany Dick, we don't experience its reality in our day-to-day lives. We live in a part of the world that celebrates the three B's—beauty, brains, and bucks—and the three P's—power, perfection, and productivity.

Though we know that God's values are at odds with this world's, many of us are unconsciously swayed by the culture of celebrity, power, and influence. When that happens, we begin to believe God can't really use us unless we have our act together. We start to feel we're ineffective unless we're sharp and successful, thin and thriving, living the "victorious Christian life"–or seeming to–like the handful of headliners who speak at Christian conferences, write successful books, and pastor the megachurches.

God longs to set us free from that boxed-in thinking. He loves us! He takes great pleasure, as He always has, in using weak, flawed, eccentric, failed human beings to highlight His power. That way onlookers won't mistakenly give anyone else the credit due God alone.

Think of just a few of the clay pots in the Scriptures:

- Moses had a fear of public speaking and problems with anger management.
- Sarah was caught laughing behind the door–no doubt at Abraham–at an inappropriate moment.
- Jonah ran away from God and became whale vomit.
- The apostle Peter seems never to have had an unexpressed thought.
- Youth group member Eutychus is remembered solely because he fell right out the window when the apostle Paul's sermon went on too long.

These people weren't perfect saints. They were flawed humans, just like us. And all were used powerfully by God.

The Delightful Decade

When Dick came to the end of himself, he realized the beginnings of God's power. The next ten years became a decade of miracles.

Ginny got well. The church exploded with new growth. Dick started that little breakfast gathering on Thursday mornings that grew to about 375 men, including many nonbelievers.

Meanwhile, Dick was in great demand all over the East Coast and renowned in the Tidewater area—especially after he started appearing as a weekly guest on the area's most popular daytime talk show.

The hostess liked Dick's humor and practical ideas. So she took the unprecedented step of inviting Dick to appear on the show once a week for six weeks to discuss the Bible—which is not exactly the kind of thing that happens to most pastors or on most television talk shows.

Six weeks turned into *ten years* of weekly televised Bible teaching. When Dick asked the man who directed the program why in the world the station was not only hosting Dick but also paying his church a talent fee, the guy paused for a minute. "You're low-key," he told Dick. "You're conversational. You're not preaching or threatening."

"The very characteristics that made me a voice mumbling in the wilderness back in Bible school gave me this extraordinary opportunity to share the Bible on secular TV," Dick says today. "The audience was mostly women, and they all ran their husbands right into the Thursday morning Bible study. It was beautiful. I saw firsthand how God used my 'inadequacies' for His purposes."

> *"If we will admit our inadequacy, we can have God's adequacy.... The greatest problem in the church is trying to do God's work with man's strength.... The key to Christian sufficiency is realizing that everything comes from God and nothing comes from me."*
>
> **Ray Stedman**

Dick's crisis on the nursery floor had turned into a lifestyle. "I can't," he would say to himself, confronted with challenges large and small. "But He can!" God was working through Dick, even through his habitual fear of failure and consciousness of his own inadequacies. And great things were happening.

Now, if this was the kind of cheerful, victorious Christian-life story one sometimes hears, that would be the end of the story. All nice and tidy. Lessons learned, tied up in a box with a lovely, status quo bow.

But no. Even then, the storm clouds had begun to gather.

As you know, Dick's health began to fail. He was jogging one summer morning when his legs went spastic. He rested a while, until the shaking went away.

Day after day, the pattern repeated, but he refused to stop jogging. Sometimes when he was running–sort of–he looked so pitiful that strangers would pull to the side of the road and beg him to let them give him a ride.

His doctors couldn't find a cause. It must be stress, they thought. They suggested that Dick slow down a little.

Dick's big, successful church could now afford to give him a year's sabbatical, during which time he and Ginny sensed God leading them to shepherd another church without quite so many demands. They moved and took on the leadership of the small Williamsburg Community Chapel in Williamsburg, Virginia.

Things went well at the new church, but Dick's physical symptoms went downhill. Bit by bit, over the next ten years, his physical abilities were taken away. First legs, then trunk, then arms and upper body. Paralyzed.

When he was an active pastor on the fast track, he had two young people in his congregation who were quadriplegics. One had broken her neck in an automobile accident, and Dick began to meet with her for Bible study once a week. Her father was a retired naval aviator who sternly told Dick that he should never, ever cancel an appointment with her because it took him four hours to get her ready.

The young woman came to faith in Christ. When Dick baptized her, it was the first time he had picked up a quadriplegic. He was shocked by the physical sensation of lifting her–she had no control over her muscles, and lifting her was like picking up 110 pounds of marshmallows.

The other young person had broken his neck water skiing the day after high school graduation. Dick grew close to both kids and felt he knew something about what it was like to live with their limitations. Now, as he looks back, he says he had no idea at all.

"Imagine what it's like," says Dick, "to be completely immobile, your arms like thousand-pound bricks by your sides. Now imagine what it feels like to know that there's a wasp in the room...."

Such helplessness demands help. In Dick's case, his wife, Ginny, has been caring for him for nearly twenty years with no days off, no vacations, and she is never away from Dick for more than an hour or two.

Dick used to call Ginny his "caretaker," and then he called her his "caregiver," which seemed more accurate. Now he calls her his "carelover," because it takes a supernatural, pure fruit-of-the-Spirit love to do all the things she does.

A Day in the Life of Dick and Ginny

The Woodwards' day begins with medications at about five o'clock in the morning. After this, Ginny has an hour of prayer and Bible reading. Then she comes back to the bedroom and turns on the stereo system, cranking it up with worship music like the Brooklyn Tabernacle Choir, Maranatha Praise songs, and church choirs with enormous pipe organ accompaniment.

Thus fortified, the Woodwards rock and roll with worship and song as Ginny gives Dick a bed bath. (Saturday is shower day when Ginny wheels Dick into a drive-in shower, like a carwash.)

Ginny then puts Dick's socks, jogging pants, and tennis shoes on him. She places a nylon sling under his body. This hooks to a hydraulic hoist. By pumping the hoist, she raises Dick up from his bed like a sack of oats and lowers him into his wheelchair.

Ginny then rolls Dick into the bathroom, washes his hair in a hospital sink, and blows it dry. She uses a special electric toothbrush on his teeth. She shaves him. She dresses him, and then she wheels him into his study for his devotional time.

Then Ginny gets dressed herself, prepares breakfast, and feeds it to Dick. Then she lies down on the couch for a while to recover.

This regimen requires somewhere between two and three hours every day. (Now Dick understands why it took that father four hours to get his daughter ready for her appointments with him.) After a time of prayer together, Ginny wheels Dick into the living room, brings in the hoist, and transfers him to the hospital bed there.

At this point, Dick usually works for hours on his voice-activated computer, creating study booklets, sermons, and Mini Bible College materials. By late afternoon, he usually takes appointments. Though he no longer counsels, per se, he mentors several young men, meeting with each on a regular basis.

The Woodwards' home is a Williamsburg hotspot. Students, pastors, friends, and visitors from all over the world find their way there. They don't visit out of a sense of dry duty to the poor handicapped pastor. People want what the Woodwards have. (As one college kid put it, "Dick rocks!")

Think about the miracles at work here. First, by means of this handicapped man, helpless in a hoist, four billion people have the opportunity to hear the Gospel on the radio each day. Listeners around the world have no idea that the man who gives them biblical hope and truth cannot move a muscle. Listeners who hear Dick's teachings and read his booklets would be amazed to see just what it takes for this man to produce so faithfully.

Second, Dick and Ginny's serenity is amazing. How easy it would be to fall into bitterness and despair! Instead they overflow with the fruit of God's Spirit: *real* love, *real* peace, *real* joy. As they would say, it's because they have made themselves available to be filled by the Giver of such good gifts. God has worked, and continues to work, supernatural miracles in their lives. They say their marriage has never been better; never have they been more content.

Dick leads a more active, fulfilled life than most able-bodied people I know. His dramatic physical disability has served as a showcase for *God's* ability.

Here's the point. If Dick and Ginny can overflow with God's presence in their lives, then you and I can too. It begins with realizing that we are empty pots apart from Him... and asking Him to fill us up. "For in Christ all the fullness of the Deity lives in bodily form, and you have been given fullness in Christ" (Col. 2:9-10).

On the Air

Dois

Bonaire is a flat, rocky island north of Venezuela, part of the Dutch Antilles. Its clear, blue waters are home to some of the best diving and snorkeling in the Caribbean. Thousands of neon flamingos patrol the shimmering coast near the Solar Salt Works, one of the largest salt production plants in the western hemisphere.

This colorful setting is about as far away from Dick Woodward's black wheelchair as one could imagine. So it's no surprise that in God's paradoxical way of doing things, Bonaire was His location for the first international radio transmission of the Mini Bible College.

In the late 1960s, Trans World Radio (TWR) realized that the Caribbean—and specifically, Bonaire—was the best strategic broadcasting location to reach South America for Christ. As they negotiated for land on Bonaire, they found they had friends in high places. It turned out that Queen Wilhelmina of the Netherlands had come to know a man from the Fellowship Foundation named Wallace Haynes. He had talked with her about Christ, and she had been receptive. So she liked TWR's plan to broadcast the Gospel from the Dutch island of Bonaire–so much, in fact, that she leased TWR the use of the land for a dollar a year.

God Multiplies Resources

It turned out that the island was one of the most efficient locations on the entire planet to build radio towers. Why? Because the extremely high concentration of solar salt on Bonaire–surrounded on four sides by salt water–provided incredible conductivity for the radio waves. Transmission strength was roughly *doubled* by the salty location.

Isn't that just like God? He takes material assets and reproduces them, multiplying resources far beyond what we could have dreamed for an *eternal* return on investment.

As we started doing radio and asking God to lead us to new opportunities, I saw that divine multiplication factor at work again and again. The next place I saw it most clearly was in the dynamic, diverse nation of India.

Passage to India

In 1986, soon after we got Dick's teaching launched from Bonaire, a friend invited me to India. I had no idea that the trip would become the next step in our ministry of broadcasting and church building.

Having never been to India before, I was fascinated by the stories of friends who had served there as missionaries. It seemed such a mysterious, diverse, and culturally rich land.

My fascination ebbed slightly, however, when I saw the conditions there. In the cities, where we traveled by taxi, the impassable, impossible roads were clogged with bicycles, throngs of people, rickshaws, old cars, elephants, swarms of flies, and sacred cows. It seemed that everything except the elephants and the flies had horns, and the cacophony of blowing, tooting, blasting, blaring, honking, and shouting was deafening.

As we traveled away from the clamor of the cities, the villages assaulted our senses in a different way.

My friend Jack took me to Vijayawada and a number of other unpronounceable locations in southern India. We jolted and bounced our way over deeply-rutted dirt roads. It was January in the southern hemisphere, so the sweltering summer heat had not yet swept across India's plains, but even so, the jeep raised clouds of red dust that filled my throat and covered my face.

My first impression of the villages was of the acrid smell of smoke from open fires. There were no toilets, and in the morning the people would walk out from the main part of the village, each carrying a small pot of water. With this they would find a spot to do their morning constitution and then wash themselves.

Their huts had thatched roofs and sides, with closely packed dirt floors swept so briskly that they shone. They were about fourteen-by-fourteen feet. Everything that we do in the various rooms of our comfortable homes–preparing food, eating, washing, sleeping, you name it–took place, for these Indian families, in that tiny space.

One or two water buffalo were usually parked outside the huts. They were used for milk, as well as pulling wooden carts. In some places, the villagers eat their meat. I'm hoping that they marinate it a good, long time, since I can't imagine anything much tougher than a hefty slab of water buffalo.

The buffalo's most significant contribution each day is its dung. The women collect the droppings by hand, shape them into patties and lay them out in the sun to dry. Then they use the dried dung patties as we would use charcoal briquettes for the barbecue. If you walk into the village in the early morning or late afternoon, the smoke and haze from the dung fires hang low over the whole village. It's a smell you never forget.

Immense Need

There are about 600,000 villages like this across India. Six hundred and fifty million people live in these villages. That's more than twice the population of the United States. Naked children play outside, their diseases untreated, their life expectancy low, and their spirits unnourished. Hinduism is the predominant belief system, and in many villages that means the worship of thousands of household gods–little manmade idols like something out of the Old Testament.

I thought about the situation in those villages and compared it with my own comfortable home where my physical needs were met in every possible way and my spiritual blessings overflowed. I knew that much is required of those to whom much is given, but practically speaking, how could *I* help millions of people in India?

Such staggering human distress can make me feel stymied. If I can't fix it, then why try helping at all? What good can my small efforts really accomplish?

But both my business experience and my faith told me that small beginnings lead to greater ends. I got excited when my friend Jack told me that you could build a church in an Indian village for as little as $5,000. Because the people do most of the work themselves–digging the footings, making the sun-dried bricks, building the walls–you could, for that sum, construct a twenty-by-forty-foot building. Eight hundred square feet.

Since the Indians typically sit on the floor–men on one side, women on the other–you could fit about two hundred people in a little church like that. A spiritual home for two hundred, a physical place for them to gather, hear the Gospel, and bring their neighbors. What a great investment!

I explored the idea with Dr. Joshua, a Christian leader I met through Jack. Dr. Joshua connected me with a member of his congregation who was a builder–and we got to work. I funded a church building in honor of my dad, Rosser Memorial Baptist Church. Was I a Baptist? No. Was the church Baptist? No. That's just what the Indians wanted to call it.

A few months later I came back to India to build another church as a memorial to my mother, then another one for my older brother, who had just died. Within a short time I had been able to fund eight churches through a partnership with Dr. Joshua and another two churches through Asia for Christ, an indigenous Indian mission group.

Building churches is like eating peanuts: once I started, I couldn't stop.

"I Prayed for Twenty Years"

In the village where we built one of the first churches, the Hindus had sneered at the Christians for years. "If your God is so great," they jeered, "why does He not even have a temple?" The Christians had explained that God's temple dwells in human hearts, but still, they yearned for a physical place to gather as a group and demonstrate that spiritual reality.

The day we dedicated that village church, a tattered old man grabbed my arm. Dr. Joshua translated as he spoke: "I prayed for twenty years," he said, his dark face split by a huge grin. "I prayed that a church would come to our village. It would take a miracle for that to happen. And now here it is!"

Within two years we had to add a second story to that church, doubling its capacity. And as time went on, I saw how these simple sanctuaries had an incredible impact on their communities. As people came to know Christ, they reached out to their neighbors. Men stopped abusing alcohol and mistreating their families. Women cared for one another. The little churches hosted classes where village boys and girls–and adults–learned to read. People were freed from the tyranny of little man-made gods.

One at a Time

I began to have a vision that freed me from the paralysis that can come in the face of overwhelming need. I saw that, huge as India was, *this* was how whole nations could be changed– person by person, community by community, state by state. After all, through the centuries, the Gospel has always worked through the power of the One who transforms human lives– *one by one by one.*

One time Jack Eckerd, the colorful founder of the Eckerd drugstore chain, came with us to India. I'll never forget this tall, outspoken lion of the corporate world, in his seventies at the time, striding along a dusty village path with a whole train of ragged little kids following him as though he was the Pied Piper.

Jack Eckerd funded a number of churches in India. He was fond of telling the story of a little boy who was walking the beach after a huge storm. The big waves had washed thousands of starfish up onto the sand.

The boy stooped, picked up a dying starfish, and flung it into the surf. Then he rescued another. And another. And another.

An old man watched him from a beach chair.

"Son, why are you doing that?" he called out. "There're thousands of starfish stuck on the beach! You can't make a difference when there are so many!"

The boy bent, picked up another starfish, and threw it into the water.

"Did you hear me, boy?" shouted the old man. "It won't make any difference!"

The boy flung another starfish into the sea.

"Well," he said, "it makes a difference to that one."

A Vision Grows

So I got fired up about building churches. I kept running back and forth to India–not an easy commute–and whether abroad or at home, I began to walk with a new sense of wonder. I saw how Christ was drawing men and women to Himself and how He used little church buildings as sanctuaries for new believers to grow.

In 1987, I returned to India with a friend, Burt Reed. Burt is a kind, comfortable pastor with an easy laugh. He had been with Trans World Radio for many years and had shepherded churches in the U.S. His pastor's heart worked well with my business head. We went to a Christian conference in Vijayawada, where about 120 Indian church leaders shared their hopes and dreams. We all prayed for God's leading.

Burt and I saw the commitment of these rural pastors as they held meetings under canopies of bamboo leaves. We both had a vision of the incredible ways the Kingdom might expand if pastors like this had encouragement, additional Bible training, and the money to build facilities in which their congregations could gather and grow.

At the end of that trip, I committed money to build five more churches. But I wanted to do something bigger than what I could accomplish alone.

Burt and I brainstormed how to help. We could see the elements of how churches could grow and reproduce themselves. The first tool was radio. Imagine the potential if Dick Woodward's teaching, now captured on tape, was translated into India's many languages and beamed across that huge nation! Listeners could learn about Christ and then come together with other believers in their area. They could form Bible studies under a pastor's leadership.

Then they would need a physical place to worship, teach the Word, take the sacraments, and have fellowship–a church building. That new congregation would then plant other congregations in nearby villages.

As a businessman, I could see the rollout in my mind; the multiplying potential was absolutely staggering.

God Calls a Meeting

So in January 1988, Burt and I returned to India. We were like Abraham, or hobbits, as Ellen would say: we had no idea how our journey would end. All we had were the names of five Christian leaders in India, given to us by Leighton Ford and other friends. We wanted to pull together an advisory group of Indians to help us strategize how God might use us in their great nation.

The only problem was that none of these men knew Dois Rosser from a hole in the wall–and this was before the days of the Internet and instant email introductions.

Burt and I flew into Madras (now Chennai), in southwestern India. I called the first person on my list. I felt ridiculous. "My name is Dois Rosser," I began, "and you don't know me, but I have an idea that may help many in India come to Christ."

That probably sounded grandiose, but my listener was kind enough to let me continue.

My next sentence was no better. "I don't mean to trouble you, but I'm wondering if you could possibly get on a plane and meet us in Bangalore to discuss all this?"

That was the equivalent of calling someone who lived in Chicago and asking him or her to meet you in Norfolk. Sight unseen.

Well, God was calling His people together, not me. Against all human odds, the next thing I knew, Burt and I were sitting at a hotel conference table in Bangalore, India, with all five of the busy individuals we had contacted. All were leaders of the highest caliber, people of vision, leadership skills, and deeply rooted spiritual maturity.

Only God could have orchestrated such a meeting–and the partnerships that were to grow from it.

God Multiplies Resources

Just as the salt on Bonaire doubles the radio transmission of the Gospel, God takes our stuff and multiplies it. When we move forward in faith and give the little we have to God, He enlarges it in ways we could not have dreamed of.

Consider this example. Alexis is a friend who was very tight in one particular resource–like most of us, she was short on time. She is a single mom. Her husband left her for another woman when her two boys were young, so Alexis and the boys had to move from their comfortable home to a cramped townhouse. She went back to work.

By the time the boys were teenagers, Alexis was tired all the time, but she and the boys now lived in a good home in a great neighborhood. She had steadily climbed the corporate ladder at her telecommunications company. Between her long work hours and managing the home and the boys' sports and school and music schedules, her days and nights were absolutely packed.

Except Sunday nights.

That was Alexis' night. While the boys were at church youth group, she'd eat a pint of Rocky Road for dinner, do laundry, and try to catch up.

Then came the crisis. One of the couples who led the youth group had just had a handicapped baby and had to resign. The director came to Alexis. Could she help?

Oh, God! Alexis prayed. *Isn't there somebody else? My plate is already full.*

In the end, though, she felt God nudging her to take the plunge and trust Him. There went Sunday nights.

Oddly enough, though, ever since Alexis gave up those Sunday nights, she's had more time than before. After she'd been meeting with some of the senior girls for a few months, they gave her a creative birthday present. They started cleaning her house every Thursday night while Alexis took her boys to band practice. Aside from that miracle, however, Alexis couldn't quite put her finger on why her time expanded rather than diminished.

One thing she knew: Sunday nights gave her energy rather than draining it. The kids who graduated and moved on would call to encourage her. They prayed for her. The ministry became a two-way street.

Today Alexis's sons have graduated from college. She is as busy as ever. But she still gives her Sunday nights to that youth group. And God still multiplies her time.

.

Concrete Realities

Dois

After we met with the Christian leaders in India, I sat down early one morning with another cup of coffee and a bigger yellow pad than I had used before. I prayed about the future. I felt as though God was edging me out of business-as-usual and into something new.

It had happened gradually. First, God had connected me with Dick Woodward and led us to put Dick's Bible teaching on the radio. Then He had taken me to India to see believers who needed help. He had shown me how easy it was—relatively speaking—to build a church and thereby influence an entire community for Christ.

I took stock. I was sixty-five years old, my auto and real estate businesses were going extremely well, and I was materially blessed beyond what I ever could have anticipated.

What did God want me to do next?

Umbrella Prayers

Bit by bit I began to understand. I have always thought of God's will as a divine umbrella. When I am in communion with Christ and earnestly seek His will, I am under His authority and protection. Rarely does God lead me by direct command: *Go here, do this, turn to the left or right.* That happens occasionally, but more often God leads me in the general direction of His will, under His umbrella, as I step out.

I felt as though God had given me my business experience to equip me for this new work. Having seen the spiritual and material poverty abroad and so many places where there were no churches at all, I came to believe that local churches are the key to cultural transformation.

I began to sketch out ideas for an international ministry of radio broadcasting and church building. This wasn't particularly strategic on my part–after all, God was already making these things happen. But now was the time to figure out how to unite the work of radio with global church building, to expand our efforts so God's seed would fall on more and more foreign soil. I wanted to take the principles that had made money work hard for profit in the business world and use them to leverage our return on investment in terms of souls touched for the Kingdom.

So we founded International Cooperating Ministries. We're not a missions group. We just come alongside Christians who are already working in their own countries, but lack resources. We partner with them–not in a parental or patronizing relationship, but as true partners.

Without the Holy Spirit, such cross-cultural partnership is doomed to failure. To use an imperfect illustration, it would be like taking an American-made hairdryer to a foreign country and trying to plug it into the local electrical outlet. Foreign outlets are shaped differently, with prongs, receptacles, and designs varying from country to country. If you try to force U.S. electrical prongs into a foreign socket, they just don't fit. The dryer either blows up or refuses to work altogether. And your hair is still wet. So when you travel abroad, you take a converter and an adapter. The converter makes the power accessible; the adapter makes the appliance work in that cultural setting.

Our church-building efforts will not work unless we partner with men and women who have been converted, so the power flows directly from the Source. In each country, the church-building model works as it is adapted to that particular culture. So all the churches we build are the same in that they are for God's people, filled with the one same Holy Spirit.

And all our churches are different, reflecting the diverse cultures they're in, adapting to the needs of their particular communities.

Rollout

As the ministry got going, we hired topnotch staff people who could somehow put up with me. We rehabbed an old building. We bought computers and paper clips and telephone service and every other physical tool one needs to do the work of the spiritual Kingdom.

When we launched the Mini Bible College from Bonaire, it was broadcast in English. There were enough English speakers in the listening area to garner a tremendous response—so strong, in fact, that Trans World Radio encouraged us to take the next step by translating Dick's teaching into Spanish and Portuguese.

Then, as our partnership with Indian believers grew, we began translating Dick's teaching into languages like Telegu and Oriyan. We printed Dick's radio scripts in whatever languages we broadcast in. Listeners from remote villages requested these; native Christians visited them and led them to Christ. Gradually new groups of believers began to form in areas that had no existing church—when they grew to one hundred baptized believers, they applied to us for funds to build a church. And within a few years, we found ourselves broadcasting and building churches in places we never could have imagined, like Russia, China, and Vietnam.

We are always vigilant on the point that new believers be discipled in sound biblical teaching, so they'll be able to discern truth from error and won't fall under the influence of cults and heresy. So as the years have gone by, we've continued to adapt our strategies to fit the needs of the diverse nations in which we work.

In some nations, for example, radio is no longer the best way to get to broad groups of people. We've developed a targeted media approach, using CDs, cassettes, Internet streaming . . . whatever works best to get the Bible training of the Mini Bible College into the hearts and minds of believers. We're working to develop small-group studies and leaders' material that can be used in believers' homes.

In our initial test of this approach in India, 900 small groups were established in five states–providing an organized method for gathering Christians during the week to study the Word, pray, and grow together in the Scriptures. With our initial success, we anticipate that those first 900 small groups will grow into thousands more in the months and years ahead.

In a number of locations that don't have access to Internet or other means, we're using a solar-powered iPod-like gadget with built-in speakers. They are inexpensive devices loaded with devotional material in mp3 format. We're distributing them through our national partners, who pass them on to groups of 10-12 believers to be trained in their own languages through Bible study material on topics like "marriage and family," a "survey of the Scriptures", and "a prescription for peace" in everyday life.

Going Where God Leads

People often ask me, "How do you get involved in these different countries? How do you find the entrees?"

My answer is always the same: *"We go where God leads us."*

There is no other way that we could even begin to attack some of the opportunities that have come our way.

For example, we thought about building churches in Cambodia a few years ago. We'd never been there, but it seemed strategically important in terms of proximity to Vietnam and the tremendous needs there in the wake of Pol Pot's devastation.

Then two men, Bob Roosen and Troy Wiseman, called me. The conversation went something like this: "Mr. Rosser, we understand that you build churches in various parts of the world.

We have a dream to build combination church-orphanages. We'd like to see if we could link with you to do that." So we set up a meeting.

They flew in from Colorado. Both were articulate and organized, with a deep love for the Lord. Troy had grown up in an orphanage, had done well financially, and both he and Bob had a tremendous burden to help the orphans of the world. "We'd like to build ten orphanages a year at a cost of about $25,000 each," he told me.

Well, building orphanages was not on my business plan, but I agreed to keep their idea in mind. As I traveled around the world, I'd look for opportunities.

Then I went to Cambodia. The people's suffering there was beyond what I had imagined. We met wonderful Christians, including Ted Olbrich, an American pastor, farmer, and businessman who had married Sou, a Laotian national who had a deep love for Cambodia.

Where did Ted and Sou take us?

To an orphanage. I saw the need firsthand.

In connecting us with Ted, God had brought us to the very man He had in mind, from the beginning of time, to help us carry out His work in Cambodia. I also found out that we could build a combination church-orphanage for *less* than $25,000.

Ted connected us with Norm Knudsen, leader of Children of Promise, a ministry that helps orphans around the world. Bob and Troy gave us the money to start building the orphanage facilities; other friends contributed money for the church components. Within one year of starting work in Cambodia under Ted's leadership, we had nineteen orphanages built or under construction as part of our bigger plan for a total of 104.

Could we have dreamed such a grand plan? No. Did God show it to us all at once? No. But as we stepped out under His umbrella, He connected us to Bob, Troy, Norm, Ted, Sou, and others. And then He used us, all working together, to do something wonderful.

Another example: How did God initiate our ministry in Vietnam, one of the world's last communist holdouts? Was it through the machinations of international diplomats or the State Department, or the financial backing of corporate investors?

No, we began building churches in Vietnam because of a guy named Bob Daley, an unassuming guy who worked down the street at the post office in Hampton, Virginia.

Entertaining Strangers

Bob's story starts back during the Korean War. Merchant ships crewed by Korean sailors would come into the Newport News shipyard for repair. At the time, our area didn't have much to offer any visitor, let alone those who did not speak English. The sailors were lonely, far from home, and in many cases the only places and people welcoming them were bars and prostitutes—provided, of course, they had money.

Some people in the community complained about the Korean imports. But Bob Daley remembered that the Bible says, "Do not forget to entertain strangers." One day he came to my dealership and asked if he could borrow a fifteen-passenger bus. I asked him why—had the U.S. Postal Service fallen on hard times? No, he said, he wanted to go down to the shipyard area and invite Korean sailors to our church.

So he did. Bob and his wife, Lucy, would pick up a dozen Korean sailors, bring them to church, and then farm them out to Christian families who would host them for Sunday dinner.

For two years, Bob did this, and to this day, members of our church still correspond with their Korean guests of so many years ago—as well as their children and their children's children. Lives were changed forever by those friendships that Bob's bus service made possible.

Decades went by. In the early 1970s, the U.S. was in conflict with communist forces again, this time in Vietnam. The U.S. government was bringing South Vietnamese military leaders for training at Ft. Eustis, an army base in our area, and Bob started bringing young Vietnamese officers to our church, just as he had brought the Koreans twenty years earlier.

A Heart for Vietnam

One of the young men Bob befriended was a South Vietnamese army officer named Vang Le. Vang was a believer. He and Bob formed a strong friendship and together brought many of Vang's fellow officers to Christ through the ministry of the church.

In 1971, Vang Le returned to Vietnam. When the communists took over the South in 1975, Vang went to prison for "reeducation," spending eight years of hard labor, while the authorities sought to stamp Christianity out of his heart and mind.

Although the authorities thought they had confiscated all the Bibles in the camp, for some reason they missed Vang's. At night, in whispers, he shared the Gospel with his fellow prisoners. Other pastors–detained for "reeducation" as well–echoed the Gospel message, and so the net result of the Viet Cong's sequestering so many for so long was that they provided a great opportunity for the Church to grow. In God's great irony, many, many prisoners came to know Christ in that communist camp.

In 1982, Vang Le was released, and in 1991, he made his way back to Virginia. Taking various gardening jobs, he went to Bible college and was eventually ordained as a minister.

One day in 1993, as I sat in my dealership office, Bob Daley stopped by. With him was his friend Vang Le. They sat down, and we chatted for a minute, but obviously Bob had something on his heart. He finally burst out, "Dois, can you help Vang? We've heard that people are hearing the Gospel in China because of the Mini Bible College being translated into Mandarin. Can you guys do that for the people of Vietnam?"

I had not thought about Vietnam before then–we had no contacts there, and the government was an unusually tough nut to crack. But I was moved by Vang Le's deep love for his country. Vang, out of his limited salary, was sending $50 a month to his old church, and he told me that as far as he knew, no church had been built in Vietnam since the communists had taken over Saigon in 1975.

Building churches in Vietnam wasn't exactly what I had in mind, but I had learned to try to participate with what *God* might be doing by not trying to pin Him to *my* little agenda.

At that time, Burt Reed was just getting ready to leave for India. I called him at home. "Burt," I asked, "can you get a visa into Vietnam?"

Burt didn't miss a beat. "I'll try."

In those days, the Vietnamese government just was not handing out visas easily, and Burt couldn't get one before he left, but by God's grace and the help of friends in high places, we finagled one for him.

Burt finished his business in India, picked up his visa in Bangkok, and the next thing he knew, he was in Ho Chi Minh City and driving a couple of hours south to the old church in Vinh Long where Vang Le had heard the Gospel as a child. It was a big building, but it was falling apart. Termites had eaten the studs, rain had worn the foundation, and winds had ripped the roof. As Burt talked with the pastor, his heart overflowed with the congregation's love for Christ and their desire to draw others to Him.

There was no way the communist government was going to grant that church a building permit.

But after much prayer, the "impossible" permit was granted. We loaned the money for the church to be rebuilt.

I went to Vietnam while that church was under construction. I saw church women mixing mortar in mud up to their knees. I saw men climbing flimsy ladders to lay more bricks. To get money for construction, women sold their earrings, wedding rings, bracelets, and watches. Men sold their much-prized electronic equipment, and the pastor sold his only means of transportation, his motorbike.

And He Shall Reign Forever and Ever...

We returned to Vietnam when that large, beautiful church was dedicated. Thousands of people packed into the building. We all sang hymns of gratitude to God, and members gave their testimonies. Then there was a hush. With a swish of the light fabric of their new robes, the choir rose and the piano keys thundered the opening chords of the "Hallelujah Chorus."

As we stood and listened to that incredible outpouring of praise to God, tears streamed down my face. In a land of such sorrow, a country where communist leaders still sat in positions of power, this part of the Body of Christ was proclaiming the King of Kings and Lord of Lords, the One who will reign forever, regardless of what human governments rise or fall.

Hallelujah!

Today that Vinh Long church has planted more than thirty-six other congregations, and we are building many more churches in Vietnam. Again, this incredible exponential growth in a closed communist state began because God worked through one man. Not a charismatic international leader but a person who would not stand out in a crowd, Bob Daley. As Scripture says, God uses the "weak" things of this world to shame the wise. He works through anyone who is wholly abandoned to Him–and He will use His people to transform individual lives as well as nations.

Entertaining Strangers

Bob Daley had no idea God would use him to build churches in a communist country. He just knew there were strangers in his hometown, people who were far from their own homes. So he welcomed Korean sailors for chicken potpie on Sundays and then did the same for South Vietnamese officers.

The Bible says to entertain aliens among us–which, in twenty-first century America, is not hard. People from other cultures are all around us. We just need to come out of our box to connect with them.

Our friend Lucy was at Home Depot one day, shopping for a ceiling fan, when she heard a commotion. A boy about ten years old, evidently autistic, was shrieking and throwing himself around wildly in a full-fledged tantrum. His mother, a slender Muslim woman in flowing robes that covered her from head to toe, had a young toddler in her orange cart. She was embarrassed, frantic, and unwilling to leave her toddler to chase after the bigger boy.

Lucy stepped up to the cart. "May I help you?" she asked. "I'll watch the little one while you get the other...."

The woman looked at her, discerned the bond of a fellow mother, and nodded. "Thank you," she said.

Later, when things were calm again, Lucy learned the women's name: Adaiya. She was from the other side of the world and lived in Lucy's neighborhood. Her husband was in government work, and they were in the D.C. area temporarily.

After the Home Depot episode, Lucy saw Adaiya in the neighborhood, walking the baby in a stroller, her chador flowing behind her. The juxtaposition of the ancient clothing and modern conveniences always surprised Lucy. She'd wave at Adaiya as she drove by, surprised as well by the young woman's earnest joy to see her.

When summer came Lucy and her friends loved late afternoons at the neighborhood swimming pool. The kids would all play together in the water and the women would laugh and talk and tease each other about what they were going to make for dinner. Often they'd just end up calling Dominos and having pizzas delivered to the pool.

Then Adaiya started showing up, though at the far side of the pool, across from where Lucy and her friends made their camp. She'd dangle the toddler off the edge while the autistic son splashed in the water. And she still wore the chador.

"At home we have separate swimming pools," she explained later to Lucy in her precise English. "The men use one, the women another. Then we can wear bathing suits. But here, where it's mixed, I must be covered."

It was easy to hang out with her girlfriends, but Lucy made herself cross the line each day. Adaiya was like a flower opening before her interest. As the summer went by, Lucy told her about Jesus–not the remote prophet, forerunner of Mohammed, but the Friend who walked with her all the time.

Just before the start of the new school year Lucy went to her mailbox one day. There was a small box and a note from Adaiya. In the box was an intricate silver necklace, and Adaiya's note said that her husband's assignment in the U.S. had ended. "We are returning home," Adaiya wrote. "It will be good to be back with my family. But I will always treasure our time in the U.S. because of you. You made me welcome. You were my friend. Because of you, I began to think that Jesus could be a Friend too."

A few weeks later Lucy opened the *Washington Post*. Near the end of Section A was a photo of the leader of a middle eastern nation. Next to him was Adaiya's husband–the new minister of the interior for that Muslim country.

Hiccups and Snorts

As we try to listen for God's leading, the work He has for us to do doesn't always proceed as smoothly as we would like it to. We need patience. It reminds me of a lawn sprinkler. You drag out your garden hose, uncoil the kinks, hook up the sprinklers, place them where they're needed, and walk back to the house to turn on the water. The water snorts in the line; then the sprinkler jerks and spurts a little water and a few hiccups of air. Then nothing. But as the water fills the hose, the stream flows, and the sprinkler blows, raining water on the parched grass.

As we pray and walk down the path God has prepared for us, it is as though He turns on a hose. There are a few hiccups and snorts, but then this thing that God is doing begins to flow. That is how it happened with International Cooperating Ministries. Before we even knew what was happening, we saw water raining down and new churches growing all over the place.

As time went on, I would be in Cuba one month and Zimbabwe the next. Sometimes Shirley went with me. At home we were still involved in all our business ventures and serving the various parachurch ministries we loved, like Prison Fellowship and others. I taught Sunday School. Shirley served in leadership for our local Community Bible Study group, which discipled about 350 women every week. We continued our normal lives.

But then Shirley and I did something we've been told is not so normal.

The Real Inheritance

Dois

On a beautiful April weekend in 1993, I booked a reservation for eight at the Homestead hotel in the mountains of Virginia. The woods were laced with fresh new leaves; the purple red-bud, daffodils, and cherry trees were heavy with blooms. It was Shirley's birthday, and much to my amazement I had been able to make arrangements for a surprise celebration–without Shirley finding out about our plans.

Shirley and I were relaxing in our room on Friday evening when there was a rap on the door. "Can you get that?" I asked innocently, and Shirley opened the door to find our children and their spouses–Pam and Gary, Cindy and Burt, Janice and Bob–all shouting, "Surprise!" and, "Happy birthday, Mom!" We had a great time toasting and roasting Shirley for the rest of the weekend. We played golf and tennis, ate too much, and enjoyed the opportunity to be together without interruptions.

But as wonderful as it was, there was more on the weekend's agenda. Shirley and I had come to some key decisions about our estate, and I wanted to make sure that the rest of the family was on board. On Saturday morning we consumed an enormous breakfast, delivered to our room so we could have privacy. After eggs, bacon, sausage, biscuits, orange juice, and several gallons of coffee, I stood up, cleared my throat, and told everyone that Shirley and I had something we wanted to discuss.

They quieted down. As I started talking in a vague way, I could see our daughters shooting glances at one another, as if they thought Shirley and I were going to announce that we were having another baby or that we had decided to run away with the circus.

I spoke of our economic situation. When the girls were growing up, we had been financially comfortable but not unusually well-off. Since they had grown, however, our investments and businesses had done really well–our estate, in fact, was now worth a good deal more than they would have ever guessed. The topic wasn't something that came up in everyday conversation.

I kept beating around the bush, hemming and hawing, trying to acquaint our daughters and sons-in-law with the scope of our holdings without getting into specific numbers.

I was confident about God's leading, that He was guiding Shirley and me toward a radical decision, but now, looking at my daughters' upturned faces, I quailed. I didn't know of any way to soften what they might consider to be a blow.

Then Cindy came to my rescue. "What is it, Dad?" she asked gently. "Go ahead. What's on your mind?"

I took a deep breath. "What I'm trying to say is: How would you feel if your mother and I took our entire estate and put it into building churches and broadcasting the Mini Bible College around the world–rather than willing it to you as your inheritance?"

The words were out. I felt miserable.

Pam, Cindy, and Janice all looked at me, their lovely faces perplexed.

Oh, no, I thought. *They feel left out. Abandoned.*

But then I realized the real reason for their confusion. I'm not sure which one spoke the actual words. I only recall that they all nodded in agreement.

"Oh, Dad," they said, smiling. "Is that all? We never thought of it as *our* inheritance! Tell us more!"

So much for preliminaries. With the tension broken, we went on to discuss the whole arrangement. We laughed. We cried. And I saw that God had blessed us in ways we could never begin to measure—in terms of the wealth of wisdom our daughters had somehow accrued along the way.

Countercultural

Each daughter responded in keeping with her particular personality. Cindy, the pastor-theologian, said, "Maybe it's countercultural not to expect the wealth of parents to be passed on, but I've always believed that financial blessings are meant to become blessings to others. Particularly those in special need." She went on, warming to the subject. "My true inheritance—the one I've valued as an exquisite gift—has been the model of your love for Christ and how you've lived that love in a way that is concrete and compassionate and in line with the Great Commission. That's my *real* inheritance! That's what I want to pass on to my own children!"

"Right," Janice agreed. "I never had any expectation that your estate was ours. I mean, think about it—you made us work so hard growing up; we never had a chance to take it easy and assume anything would be handed us!"

She was teasing, but Shirley and I grinned as we thought back to the girls' teen years. A lot of other kids at their schools drove nice cars. You would think, since I was in the car business, that they would have sharp little sports cars to drive themselves to cheerleading practice. But I never wanted them to have a sense of entitlement. I did give them a car—a '56 Chrysler convertible that went from zero to sixty in about two days. I called it "basic transportation." They called it "the White Bomb."

It was the same with clothes. I was amazed at the absolute horrors of high school girls ever wearing the same thing twice. When the girls moaned about needing something, Shirley would tell them, "You know, we can buy one or two for you... but you don't need an entire closet full of those things. It's important that you earn money to buy things for yourself."

All three of them knew they were expected to hold part-time jobs in high school and college. They all worked at the car dealership; Pam was a receptionist, Cindy did inventory in the parts department, and Janice filed receipts and records and reports until her eyes crossed. In the process, the girls developed a healthy work ethic. As they watched the decisions Shirley and I made from the time they were toddlers, they had absorbed more than I had realized.

"Dad," Janice said as we continued our discussion at the Homestead, "you're acting as if this is some big surprise. To us, it's the most natural thing in the world. You and Mom have acquired your resources through your own hard work.... It's yours to do with as the Lord directs you! Besides, it all belongs to God anyway, right?"

Pam, our eldest daughter, an elementary school teacher, held back for a while, uncharacteristically quiet. I realized she had been thinking, as an adopted daughter, about what an inheritance really meant.

She leaned forward, her hands clasped in front of her, her voice catching a little. "My heavenly Father gave me an inheritance of learning about Him when He placed me in your arms," she said. "I thank the Lord daily for His parental choice. I had nothing to do with it. It blows my mind when I think of how helpless I was without a home or loved ones.... God knew me in the womb, and He granted me parents who would challenge me, hold me up when I was falling.... "

By this point we all had tears in our eyes.

"Dad and Mom," she continued, "what I mean is this: God placed me with you. All my life you've shown me His love. When I was about ten years old, I used to lie in bed and thank God for what He had given me before I was even able to ask for it. A family. An earthly father and mother who so clearly showed me the love of my heavenly Father."

"Besides," she added, changing gears, "I spend lots of time at school teaching my students about sharing. That's all this is.

What's the big deal about our family's sharing so others can hear about the love of God?"

It was nearly noon when we pushed back our chairs, clasped hands, and prayed. Being of one mind, we could not wait to see what God would do with the resources we were putting before Him.

After we formed a foundation and set up the financial arrangements to make our Homestead discussion a reality, others became aware of the thrust–though not the details–of our decisions. Some were aghast; others just shook their heads.

I am not necessarily advocating our choice for anyone else. God leads each of us in stewardship decisions. I don't know how He would choose to lead others. But I do know that Shirley and I sensed the Spirit's call in our hearts, and God confirmed that by the clear way in which He had already prepared our daughters' hearts toward the same conclusion.

Our decision has seemed strange and foolish to many people. But to the ones it directly affects–our children and grandchildren–it was the natural byproduct of perceiving, as Janice put it, that *it all belongs to God anyway.*

That *is* countercultural. It's also brought us more joy than could any material prizes like a fat 401K or a multimillion-dollar mansion. All we have to do is think of the thousands of human beings who have had, and will have, the chance to know Jesus because the Gospel came to their village.

Our unusual estate plan does not mean that any of our descendants will have to live on the street. The grandchildren are well provided for by their own parents' hard work, and, in fact, Pam, Cindy, and Janice say that our decision has addressed one of their chief concerns about their kids. They've seen many young people who have inherited wealth and have been damaged by being given too much too easily. They know of kids who've never developed a work ethic, who have missed a sense of productive purpose, whose goals have only to do with buying things that are bigger, better, and newer than what they already have. They want their own kids to have a different perspective.

Worldwide Worldview

Most of our grandchildren have traveled abroad to help others firsthand. When he was twelve, our grandson Grant traveled with his father (an ophthalmologist) and me to Bolivia. Now in his twenties, Grant says the trip changed his perceptions: "I remember chilly nights on a small cot in an Andes mountain village, going (or at least trying to go) to the bathroom standing on two tiles over a dank hole, harrowing car rides along tight trails, dodging llamas.... I remember helping my father while he conducted eye exams on grateful Bolivians. I remember meeting children my own age and seeing not only our similarities but actually seeing myself from their eyes–how fortunate I was! I was immersing myself in their culture, feeling, touching, and seeing true need, not just monetary or physical, but their spiritual need for something I'm not sure they even knew existed: *hope*."

Our oldest granddaughter, Amy Calfee, is a nurse. She says she saw the big picture after she went with Shirley and me to Ukraine. It was Amy's first trip outside the U.S. and she ended up in some pretty fragrant outhouses in the Ukrainian countryside. When she came home she looked at her flush toilet with a new, deep affection.

"Here at home it's so easy to get caught up in the day-to-day grind," Amy says. "You can see the devil trying to keep your attention focused on *things*. But in Ukraine I realized how we're on this earth for such a short time. I saw how the people there loved Jesus, how He was the center of their lives. I felt so grateful for all the blessings I have–every single thing!–and how I need to share those blessings. It just made me want to dive right in and do whatever I can to help more and more people come   to Christ!"

My Heart Is Your Heart

Two other grandsons, Carter and Matt, traveled to India with us when they were twelve and fourteen. One morning we were all leaving our hotel at about 5:00 A.M., and Carter saw a little Indian boy on the street. The boy and his entire family had been sleeping on the concrete with only a few thin shawls draped over them.

Carter emptied his backpack of the snacks he had brought on the trip and, motioning for the little boy to come over, loaded him up with granola bars and juice boxes. The boy trembled with excitement; the gift would feed his whole family that day.

On that same trip we went to a remote village to help the believers there dedicate their new church to the glory of God. After we sang "Alleluia" together, our voices mingling in that one word that is the same in all languages, an Indian man took my grandson Carter's hand. He placed it over his heart and said, as our interpreter translated, "We prayed for years that this church might become a reality! My heart is your heart, and your heart is mine."

As Cindy said later, "What parent would not want her son to understand the power of prayer as demonstrated by these faithful Indian believers… and who would not want their son to see how God uses His people in one part of the world to meet the needs of those in another part of the world?"

Flying Free from the Nest

One Christmas, Shirley and I received a gift that let us know that the decision to give away our children's inheritance was reaping eternal dividends.

Our kids and grandkids gathered around as we gently pulled the wrapping paper off a small wooden birdhouse–or actually, a bird church. It had a shingled roof, a steeple, and a cross over the door. Nestled inside was a sheet of heavy white paper, rolled up like a diploma. Shirley carefully unrolled it.

"A church to be built in Cuba," it read, "presented to the glory of God, in honor of Mom and Dad with love." It was signed by each of our daughters, their husbands, and their children: Pam, Gary, Cindy, Burt, Janice, Bob, Amy, Jenni, Allison, Carter, Ross, Grant, Matt, and Connor.

"We all worked to help pay for it, Granddaddy," said one of the younger grandkids. "We babysat, cut grass, did odd jobs–we all helped!"

A *church to be built to the glory of God in Cuba…*

As I looked at Pam, Cindy, and Janice, and their spouses and children, I felt as though I was tasting some of the fruit whose seeds God had planted during our weekend at the Homestead in 1993. Then we had laughed and cried and prayed together about the stewardship decision to use our estate to build churches rather than to fund our children and their children.

Now here we were, years later, laughing and crying again, this time under the Christmas tree, and I was seeing my childrens' children work hard and give sacrificially, that people in a communist country might come to know God.

Is our family perfect? No. But God has enabled us to make some choices that have been as life-giving as they are unexpected. And for us, giving away the earthly inheritance has in fact given us a clearer realization of eternal inheritance, the one He passes by His grace from generation to generation: "In His great mercy he has given us new birth into a living hope through the resurrection of Jesus Christ from the dead, and into an inheritance that can never perish, spoil or fade–kept in heaven for you" (1 Peter 1:3-4).

How We Invest
Dois

The first key to dreaming big is *trusting* God. Either we believe the Bible and bank on the fact that nothing is impossible for God, or we don't. I see no need to be timid when it comes to trusting God for big things.

Second, trusting God for big things means *thinking outside the box*. It means seeing things in a new way and being willing to perceive obstacles as opportunities.

A third key to dreaming big is *working lean*. By this I mean being a careful, wise manager of all we do.

Part of what I bring to the table—and to this book—is more than half a century of business experience. In real estate, automobiles, off-shore drilling, and other enterprises I haven't told you about, I've run a lot of businesses over the years. I've incorporated twenty-seven separate companies—large, small, and everything in between. But all of them run tight and lean. I'm not interested in large staffs, luxurious offices, or big overhead. I am interested in producing the best possible product at the lowest possible price, and when I invest in a new start-up, I'm interested in the highest possible return on my investment.

Why would I not bring the same standards to ministry? After all, none of the resources I handle are mine. They are God's. He owns everything. I am simply the steward, or administrator, of everything I've been given.

I will be judged accordingly. In the parable of the talents in Matthew 25, Jesus made it clear that however small or great the gifts we have been given, we will be judged and rewarded according to how well we use them for His glory. The master rewards the servants who multiply what He entrusted to them. He punishes the one who simply buried his assets.

God's assessment of our stewardship will not be based on *how much* we have but *how well* we manage what we have. Wastefulness, laziness, and greed are wrong, whether among rich or poor. As a steward-investor, I am to take great care in how I use resources—not just money, but time and talents as well.

Dick Woodward says that the clearest indicators of a person's true priorities are his or her calendar and checkbook. They show how we *really* invest our time and our treasure. Wasting time wastes precious capital. Being late to an appointment steals time from someone else. Not using a skill He's given me is the same as the slothful steward burying his talent in the ground.

And I will be held to account in heaven if I give my tithes and offerings to inefficient ministries that fail to maximize ministry for my donated dollar. That may sound like a severe standard to some. But as clearly as I can read my Bible, it's God's standard.

Shirley and I tithe—and give far beyond that ten percent—to our home church and to many wonderful ministries in the U.S. and abroad. Since we will one day be held accountable for those investments, we have taken care to give to organizations with tight financial accountability.

Lots of ministries will tell you all the great things they're doing, but if you press, they are reluctant to tell you what it costs to provide those services. We look for groups that are efficient enough with their stewardship of material funds to produce the maximum spiritual return for the Kingdom.

Similarly, we try to hold ourselves to a standard of maximum return on investment in our own ministry.

First, all ICM's overhead administrative costs are covered by the Rosser Foundation. So every designated dollar given for ministry goes entirely   to ministry. One hundred percent.

Second, just as in the business world, the key to maximizing return is leveraging. In its simplest form, leveraging is taking something small and using it to create something much larger. It is the key principle by which we operate.

As we've said before, our ministry works out of a cinderblock former warehouse. Our small staff runs on an incredible work ethic. The pace is tough. I am tough. Over the years people have come and gone because of the pace and the urgency that drives me.

But when a donor gives a dollar, what happens?

First, that whole dollar goes directly to ministry. No administration. Second, we work abroad through national partners who are typically executives with large ministries in their countries. They are top caliber people with years of management experience. They are not on our payroll; they are our *partners.* Because of that, the donor's dollar is boosted by their expertise and networks of influence.

In addition, the donor buys the skills, energies, and commitment of an ever-broadening pyramid of nationals: church leaders, individual pastors, the construction foremen, and all the church members who contribute their energies, enthusiasm, and experience to the building project at no cost to the donor or the ministry. This is the Body at work.

That's great, you say, but isn't there a risk in depending on partners who aren't on your payroll?

You bet.

As any market investor will tell you, increased leverage means increased risk. Risk is exposure to uncertainty–things we do not know or factors beyond our control. We evaluate risks as best we can and commit our decisions and partnerships to God's control. When we invest in obedience under His umbrella, we trust He'll multiply the return.

The word *leverage* comes from the old French word *leveour:* "to raise." A lever is a bar used as a pry by turning on a fixed point, or fulcrum. One applies force at one end, it turns on the fulcrum, and the increased power raises weight at the other end of the bar.

God is that fixed point. Our ministry is the bar that connects believers in one part of the world with Christians abroad. As we give funds on our end, their potential is increased by the leveraging power of the fulcrum. On the other end, our friends abroad are lifted up, boosted in a way they could not be on their own.

For example, friends at the Williamsburg Community Chapel gave $40,000 to build a church in Ukraine, the Mariupol Church of Christ the Savior. That church committed to build five daughter congregations. They found a prime location in a resort area on the Black Sea. Tourists come there from all over the region. Open-air meetings are held on the steps of the church, facing the sea, and hundreds of visitors have attended these evangelistic outreaches, spreading the impact of Mariupol's ministry across Ukraine and beyond.

Meanwhile, the congregation has been reaching out to street children, drug addicts, and in-area prisons, building a congregation of new believers behind those walls. The government donated a former school building to be used as a Christian orphanage for street kids.

So when the Williamsburg folks donated $40,000 to build, their investment didn't stop there. It has multiplied many times over in a variety of needy mission fields–and God smiles on their wise stewardship.

When you give to build a church, the dividends just don't stop!

Rusty Porter is a friend who flew B-52 bombers during the war in Vietnam. At the time he was a young, impressionable, red-haired airman. He remembers the long, terrible nights of bombing raids. He remembers coming back to the barracks and seeing the empty cots of those who didn't make it back. He remembers the sick feeling in his stomach as his plane's bombs fell; he tried not to think about the death and destruction they delivered to the people in the countryside far below.

Rusty's memories haunted him. Then he traveled to Vietnam with Burt, me, and others. His first trip to Southeast Asia since the war there brought up a maze of feelings and memories. Rusty visited the churches we were building and saw the strategic evangelistic outreaches of Christians all over that country. He saw how the Church is growing in spite of the communist government.

But most important, Rusty saw a way to help the land he had once bombed. Rusty and his wife, Ginny, have given generously to build a number of churches in Vietnam. They recently returned to Southeast Asia to visit some of those churches.

I wish you could have been with us to see the scene. Though Rusty is now in his sixties, his hair is still red. In his eager, earnest face you could still see the energetic young airman who first came to Vietnam thirty years earlier. One of the churches built by the Porters is a pastel building with a graceful bell tower and a cross stretching high into the jungle sky. Tears flowed down Rusty's face as he and Ginny stood in a circle with their Vietnamese brothers and sisters, holding hands, praying, and singing "Alleluia" to the glory of God.

Right now the churches in Vietnam are growing substantially each year . . . an ongoing, multiplying return on donor dollars.

Ginny Porter sums it up: "I had not realized until I stood there in front of that church that we had been able to build something that's not just for now but for years to come. I saw kids running around, smiling, and welcoming us . . . and I realized that that church will be there for them . . . and for their children's children. We are able to be a part of what God is doing–and will do–for *generations*."

Dois I Rosser
A man of vision used by God.

Dois and Shirley Rosser attending a church dedication in Tanzania, Africa.
September 2005

The Rosser family in 2004.
Top Left to Right: Gary Minter, Bob Allen, Burt Higgins, Dois Rosser
Bottom Left to Right: Janice R. Allen, Cindy R. Higgins, Shirley Rosser, Pam R. Minter

Training up the next generation.
Dois Rosser (Founder) and grandson, Matt Allen in the Forbidden City, China.

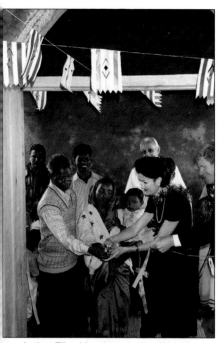

Author Ellen Vaughn cuts the ribbon to dedicate a new church in India.

Ellen Vaughn on an Amazon tributary in Peru

In the late 1980s, ICM took their first donor partners to visit churches in India.
Left to Right: Bobby Beck, Dean Woodward, Caleb West, Dois Rosser, Bob Allen

Pastor and Teacher Dick Woodward,
Author of the Mini Bible College.

MegaVoice units preloaded with three years
of Mini Bible College curriculum enable small
groups and village pastors to study the Bible
in their own language.

Cuban girls holding MBC booklets.

A small group meeting to study the Mini Bible
College in a home on a village street in India.

ICM in Asia

Chapels in Vietnam are sprinkled over the countryside.

The Church in China is growing exponentially with the church building becoming a beacon of hope to the surrounding towns and villages.

Dois Rosser with a Cambodian orphan.

Having been a part of ICM since its inception, Burt Reed travels the world to train and encourage ICM's indigenous partners. He is shown here with two children from an ICM church in Indonesia.

Orphanage and church complexes have been built by ICM and our Church Growth Partners in Cambodia. As of October 2010, 108 of these had been built, each with a capacity to provide a loving church home to 50 orphans.

ICM in Latin America

Iglesia Nuevo Eden Church in Colombia, South America

Dois and Shirley Rosser and daughter, Janice Rosser Allen (ICM Executive Chair), with Guambiano Indians, two leadership partners of Southern Colombia.

ICM in Africa

A congregation in Uganda at the dedication of their new church. Their previous church is pictured to the right

Congregation members work on the construction of their new church and orphanage, Uganda 2010.

Part 2: The Claim: "I Will Build My Church"

What Happened Next
Ellen

You can find a lot of excellent books about Christian stewardship. This is not one of them.

In fact, Dois doesn't talk a whole lot about stewardship, but as you've seen, he and Shirley live it in a radical way. Their decision to invest their estate in the work of building churches and broadcasting the Gospel was *way* outside the box. But they don't make a big deal about it. To them it was simply a que tion of following God's leading and taking a bold step in light of eternity rather than taking their direction from the values of this world.

The Rossers aren't focused on what *they did*. They're excited about what *God is doing*. Since their unconventional decision, He has multiplied their investment dramatically.

As we write, the Mini Bible College has been translated into 28 languages spoken by four billion people, and plans are in place to translate the Mini Bible College into three new languages every year.

Arabic	French (African)
Benjara	Gujarati
Bengali	Hindi
Creole	Indonesian
English	Kannada
English (African)	Khmer

Mandarin	Sora
Marathi	Spanish
Moldovan	Swahili
Nepali	Tamil
Oriya	Telugu
Portuguese	Ukranian
Punjabi	Urdu
Russian	Vietnamese

As of 2011, more than 3,800 churches have been built or are under construction, in 58 countries:

Argentina	Dominican Rep.	Malawi	Tanzania
Bangladesh	El Salvador	Mali	Tajikistan
Belarus	Egypt	Mexico	Thailand
Benin	Ethiopia	Moldova	Turkey
Brazil	Ecuador	Mozambique	Uganda
Bulgaria	Ghana	Myanmar	Ukraine
Burkina Faso	Haiti	Nepal	Uzbekistan
Burundi	Honduras	Nicaragua	Vietnam
Cambodia	India	Nigeria	Zambia
Cent. African Rep.	Indonesia	Pakistan	Zimbabwe
China	Iraq	Peru	
Colombia	Kenya	Philippines	
Congo	Kyrgyzstan	Rwanda	
Congo, DR	Kazakhstan	Russia	
Costa Rica	Madagascar	South Africa	
Cuba	Liberia	Sri Lanka	

On his office wall Dois has a big map of the world studded with pins to mark the locations of all those churches. Those hundreds upon hundreds of ordinary pinheads can move you to tears if you think of the community-changing potential of each congregation. Then you realize that each one represents at least five daughter churches . . . and in some cases, many, many more. If you have a vivid imagination, you can almost see the map on a golden wall in heaven, angels dancing on the heads of all those pins, rejoicing with each new soul who enters the fold.

The way things are going, Dois had better buy more pins.

One week before the terrorist attacks on New York and Washington, in September 2001 the Mini Bible College launched its broadcasts in Arabic. The message that day, "The God Who Is In Charge," rolled out over the Arabian Peninsula. It's a spiritual crossfire. From the north, the Gospel is broadcast on a one million-watt superstation. (Ironically, years ago the former Soviet Union constructed this station in order to flood the region with communist propaganda.) The Arabic broadcasts have also expanded via satellite radio and Internet broadcasting to cover all of Europe and North Africa.

Here's what one Arabic-speaking listener wrote to Dois after September 11, 2001.

> I want to say I am sorry to you and to all. . . . Nobody will forget what happened in the USA. If Muslims are really behind this, then it is a hit to what is called Islam.
>
> My question is, what should I do to change my religion officially? I want to change from what is called Islam to Christianity. After I read about Christ, I found Christianity to be a respectable religion. I think you can help me! My apologies and sadness again. Yours, Ahmad

Of course, Ahmad is just one person. But why not think big and dream of the day that Dois' map of the Arabian peninsula is absolutely covered with pins?

Building the Body

Ellen

Dois has written a lot in this book about building churches– individual structures with a cross on top, like the churches Rusty and Ginny Porter have built in Vietnam. But when he speaks of "the Church," he doesn't mean a building. Christ's Church is made up of *people*–people like those generations of Christian families Ginny Porter thought of when she realized who her investment was really for.

In the New Testament, the Greek word translated as "church" is *ekklesia.* It means a gathering of people called together, most commonly a public assembly of citizens, as when the people were literally "called out" of the city to vote.

Jesus first used the term in Matthew's gospel when He asked His disciples, "Who do people say that I am?"

"Some say you are John the Baptist," they told Jesus. "Others say Elijah . . . and still others believe you are Jeremiah or one of the other prophets."

"And what about you?" He asked. "Who do you say that I am?"

"You are the Christ!" said Peter. "The Son of the Living God!"

There could be no more radical statement for a first-century Jew. Peter was affirming that Jesus was Messiah.

But Jesus' response is even more significant than Peter's declaration. "Blessed are you, Simon son of Jonah," He said. "For this was not revealed to you by man, but by my Father in heaven. And I tell you that you are Peter, and on this rock I will build my church, and the gates of hell will not prevail against it. ..." (adapted from Matt. 16:13-18).

As Dick Woodward says, it's as though Christ were saying to His irrepressible friend Peter (whose name literally means "rock"), "Simon, you're not that smart! It was My Father who revealed that to you! I'm going to build My Church upon the miracle that a man like you could say something as wonderful as that, Peter! I'm going to build my Church upon the phenomenon that ordinary people will do extraordinary things because they were indwelt by the Holy Spirit. The powers of hell will not prevail against that Church, Peter, because the power within and behind that Church will be the Holy Spirit!"

So the Church is not just a nice building with a cross on top. It is Christ's "called-out people" who belong to Him.

That community of believers has different expressions. First is the *church universal,* the Body of Christ, all those whom God has called to Himself. It is made up of many traditions, denominations, and diverse cultures, and we will not all assemble together in one place until we are in heaven. We believe this is what Jesus was talking about when He said, "I will build My Church."

Then there is the *church particular.* These are the visible communities of believers who assemble in my neighborhood, and yours, in cities, towns, and villages everywhere. We gather together in local fellowships with those who worship God the same way we do—in the same language, worship style, and traditions regarding the sacraments. These are the individual congregations for whom Dois and his team are building churches all over the world.

When you visit these churches, you begin to see, just a bit, the incredible vitality of the big-picture Body of Christ. You begin to imagine what it will be like when we are all together in heaven—people of every tribe and nation, splendidly diverse, exuberantly one.

Paradoxically, one of the places we have seen that most vividly is in a small community of poor, diseased, ostracized human beings.

Living Stones
Dois

I love Paris!

I was there a while ago with Ellen and others on our way home from India. We had a six-hour layover–and after the stench and dust of Calcutta, Paris was a feast for the senses.

Our plane got in at 5:30 in the morning. We jumped on the train downtown and got off at the St. Michel stop.

It was still dark and we were cold. We looked around for a place to get breakfast. There was a café on every corner. We ducked into one, and a mustached waiter who could not possibly have been more French brought us steaming cups of café au lait and big, buttery croissants. Utterly content, I leaned back in my chair, looked out through the windows, and watched as the sun rose and lighted the immense stones of the church across the square, even as the big bells in its towers began to toll the hour.

It was, of course, the Cathedral of Notre Dame.

Workers began building that cathedral in the twelfth century. It survived the Middle Ages, the French Revolution, Nazi occupation, and all the other upheavals of history over the last nine centuries. It is an extraordinary human achievement, built to the glory of God.

But when I think of a miracle in stone, do you know what comes to my mind?

A small church in India, the remote place of worship for a handful of people who have been kicked out of their villages. They are untouchable, helpless. Against all odds, they have built a church that is a unique testimony in stone to the grace of God.

Let me tell you how we found it.

Years ago we decided to bring together our Indian pastor-partners and other friends. We rented a school in south-central India, and about 450 pastors came together. We set up extra cots in the dormitories and a big tent outside where women cooked up enormous pots of rice. Simple as it was, it was a feast of fellowship for these leaders, many of whom work without much encouragement or support.

We combined our meetings with an evangelistic appeal, and I invited Dr. Leighton Ford to speak. We also conducted seminars for Indian women as well as village outreach. In the end, thousands of people came to Christ, and our Indian pastor- partners provided discipleship and follow-up.

The Relentless Friend

One night a young Indian man came to me. "I know you've been building churches," he said. "Would you come look at a church that our congregation is helping?"

I wanted to see the church, but I was exhausted. We had been going to bed at midnight, getting up at five each morning; the days were full of ministry and the nights as well. My spirit wanted to see his church; my flesh just wanted to go to bed.

The next day, the same man was back. "Won't you come see my church?" he asked.

I put him off again. But the next day there he was again, and finally, just like the persistent widow who came after the unrighteous judge in Christ's parable, he wore me down.

"How far is it?" I asked.

"Oh, just a short drive, maybe an hour and a half from here," he said confidently.

Well, an hour and a half of Indian time can be rather different from American time.

About four hours after we started out in our beat-up jeep, bouncing and jolting over the dusty roads, we pulled into a clearing near a mountain. We parked the jeep. In the distance, up a jagged hill, I could see a clearing with the roughed-in structure of a church building.

Three large stones marked the entrance to the path up the incline. They were about ten feet high and almost as wide—irregular, heavy gray boulders. Painted on each one was a white-washed sign of the cross.

In the distance I could see people slowly making their way toward us. Acrid smoke rose from a buffalo-dung fire; in the haze I could see a few ghostly figures tending the blaze.

My Indian friend had neglected to tell me something. As we climbed the hill, I realized that I was looking at a leper colony.

I had never seen a leper before. Though the disease is unheard of in the U.S., it is still common in some tropical Third World countries.

These lepers were forced to live apart. The government had provided them a well, and they survived by begging in the nearby town, where people would fling them a few rupees from fear as much as from compassion.

It was like a scene from the New Testament. My heart twisted as I saw men and women with ragged strips of cloth wrapped around the stumps where their fingers had been. Many wore cloths over their disfigured faces. They shuffled forward to greet us, their toeless feet stirring up small clouds of dust.

As we greeted them, I realized not all were lepers. Many of the children were healthy, and so were some of the spouses. But they had been ostracized as well.

This Is the Day

As the people shyly welcomed us, our Indian friend translated: "They want you to see their church," he said.

We walked further into the little camp. As we drew closer to the church, I was thunderstruck. Still in the early stages of construction, the church was already four levels of heavy stone. The people were working together; those who were able had hacked big granite slabs out of the mountain, and the others had carried them down to build that church. I can still see them in my mind's eye; gaunt men and women edging down the mountain path on their crippled feet, cradling heavy granite boulders balanced on their fingerless hands. Then they would lay their burden on the wall, and a skilled worker would lay it in and mortar the joints.

They had been working for over a year and had no funds to continue to the next stage. Now I realized why God had brought us to that remote place–so one part of the Body could help another part.

The people stopped working and assembled to pray with us. First they sang songs of praise. I recognized the tune of "This is the day that the Lord has made; We will rejoice and be glad in it"–sung in Telegu by these lepers who were my brothers and sisters in Christ.

Suddenly a woman came through the little crowd. In her arms was a tiny baby, no more than a few hours old. Gently she placed the child in my arms, and I understood from our interpreter that she wanted us to dedicate the baby to the Lord and give her a Christian name.

As I held the child, I realized she was fiery with fever. "We need to get her to a doctor," I said. Our interpreter shook his head. "They have no money for a doctor," he said. "They just hope for the best."

The tiny child was listless. She was dehydrated. "How much does a doctor cost?" I asked.

More questions, and the translation. "Two dollars," said the translator. "They don't have it."

"We have it," I said. "Let's get this child to the doctor."

The mother motioned to me, and I realized she wanted us to pray first. I gave the baby to Burt Reed, who held her gently in his arms and dedicated her to the Lord. They named her Deborah. Then the child's parents wrapped her up and began the journey to the doctor.

Later, as we prepared to leave, the pastor of the leper colony asked if they could pray for us–and if we could pray for them. We gathered in a circle. I closed my eyes–but then, as the pastor began to pray, I heard a rustling. I looked. There, lying on the ground, their saris and shawls spread out like ragged flags, were all the members of that leper community, prostrate before the living God. As I watched them, I realized that they were no longer this world's untouchable rejects, pathetic people to be pitied. They were glad subjects of the King of Heaven.

"Once you were not a people, but now you are the people of God; once you had not received mercy, but now you have received mercy.... You are a chosen people, a royal priesthood, a holy nation, a people belonging to God, that you may declare the praises of him who called you out of darkness into his wonderful light" (1 Peter 2:10, 9).

The faith of those lepers in India was absolutely humbling. There we were, rich Americans with every resource at our fingertips–bowled over by the sight of men and women building a church with nothing at their fingertips. Not even fingers.

But that sight of weak and partial people physically moving a mountain of stone should be no surprise. It's the same paradox by which God has chosen to work since the beginning. He uses the weak and powerless things of the world to show His mighty power. He is the One who builds His church, stone by living stone.

A few years later, we returned to that church. There was no way to let our friends know that we were coming. I didn't know what we would find after we climbed the rocky hill. The little church had been finished. Triangular white banners fluttered in the breeze off its roof. The door was open. It was clean and orderly inside, empty in the middle of the day, except for the pastor. (This young man was not a leper himself–but he had been led to Christ years before by a leper he had met on the street. Out of gratitude, he now ministered to the people of this community.)

The pastor was lying on a mat on the floor, propped on his elbows, an open Bible before him. Near him a small radio was broadcasting the Mini Bible College in the Telegu language. I could not have been more delighted–until the pastor welcomed us and excitedly called down the hill for the others.

They came slowly, laboriously limping up the path, the less affected ones supporting the feebler. A small girl was helping an old woman. Then she saw us and smiled. Behind her was her mother, laughing with joy.

The little girl came running to my arms. I swept her up and hugged her tight, for I knew who she was: Deborah, the baby who had almost died.

Sometimes, back in the U.S., I used to wonder what God could do with small things. Insignificant amounts of money, little bits of time or treasure. I don't really wonder anymore, because I've seen what God did one day in 1990 with two dollars: He saved a life!

Today Deborah is a healthy young girl, in school, free of leprosy, loving the Lord.

Because that leper community is so far from my comfortable life in America, it's a touchstone for me. As I try to help believers build churches all over the world, I keep the faces of my sisters and brothers in that little colony before me.

For we are one with them. Healthy Americans, comfortable and pampered in so many ways–we are *one* with those ragged believers who live on a rocky hilltop in India.

Khakis and Nose Rings

Awhile ago we visited the Gadgaballi church somewhere in the wilds of eastern India. When Indian believers from a neighboring region first brought the Gospel to this village in the early 1980s, they found local tribal people who were mostly naked, who worshiped stones, trees, and idols.

Now, as our jeep made its way through narrow dirt trails toward this remote village, the entire congregation that has since been planted there came out to welcome us.

They were wearing their best clothes in our honor. They waved palm branches, danced to the beat of a tribal drum, and placed garlands of marigolds around our necks. A small girl came forward with a silver bowl of cool water. I dipped my dusty hands and washed them, and then a sister dried them for me with a soft towel.

According to their tribal custom, the women's faces were tattooed in black designs. Metal circlets ringed their ears; slender bones adorned their noses. They laughed as they danced around us in the red dust, their teeth shining in the sun.

I can only imagine what this would have looked like to an outsider—me, a buttoned-down white American man with khaki pants and bifocals, surrounded by exotic tribal women who were greeting me so lavishly. We could not have appeared more diverse.

Of course, we *are* very dissimilar. We look different. We speak different languages. We belong to different local churches. And believe me, we worship in very different ways. (We don't leap and dance a whole lot at the Wythe Presbyterian Church in Hampton, Virginia.)

But we are *one* in *Christ,* part of the one same universal Church of His Body, different branches springing out of the same, life-giving vine.

"I Am the Vine, You Are the Branches"

Jesus' familiar metaphor strikes me in new ways when I visit villages that are dependent on growing things. I see more clearly that He was telling His followers that they were organically connected not only to Him but also to one another. Christianity— the new Church He was founding—is not just an individual's relationship with God, wonderful as that is. It is *communal.*

"A new command I give you," He said, speaking plainly. "Love one another. As I have loved you, so you must love one another. By this all men will know that you are my disciples, if you love one another" (John 13:34).

Later, in the Garden of Gethsemane, Jesus looked ahead through the centuries to come and prayed for *us:* "My prayer is not for [the first-century disciples] alone. I pray also for those who will believe in me through their message, that all of them may be one, Father, just as you are in me and I am in you. May they also be in us so that the world may believe that you have sent me .... May they be brought to complete unity to let the world know that you sent me and have loved them even as you have loved me" (John 17:20-21, 23).

This is familiar ground. Perhaps it is so familiar that we forget its radical message. It is *our* unity, *our* oneness of spirit as believers, that validates to the watching world that Jesus Christ is the Son of God.

Here is a simple example.

There is a little church in India. Friends gave about $7,000 to build it, and when we visited the site, the believers were hard at work doing just that.

Several women, graceful in their bright saris, were mixing the mortar. They would scrape together a clump of it, pile it into a shallow tin bowl, and deftly lift the burden to their heads. Then, perfectly balanced, they would carry the load to the foundation, where the men would slather the mortar into place.

It was hard work under the blazing Indian sun. Yet these people sang, they laughed, they worked together with great contentment.

So I was not surprised when they told me what had happened next.

As the Hindus in the village watched the Christians building their church, they noticed their joy. In fact, a number were so intrigued by the believers' cooperation that they became curious about the Gospel. "How is it that you work together and care for one another in this way?" they asked. They were told about the love of Jesus, who grows Christians together. They received Him, were baptized, and became part of the church community in that village.

I could not help but wonder: how many of our neighbors in the United States have come to Christ due to the joyful *unity* exhibited in our church building programs?

Who Are We?

The Church in the world today is people, those called by the Spirit of God. We are diverse. We are one. The local expression of the Church can be in the form of believers who gather in a house in China, under a Banyan tree in India, or in a prison unit in South America–a church certainly does not need a building to be the Church.

During the past decade or so in the U.S. megachurch movement, some American Christians focused too much on facilities. Motivated by a desire to draw in nonbelievers, they concentrated on buildings and buses and basketball arenas and raising big budgets, and somewhere along the line they lost sight of the work of building up the people.

But now, perhaps, the pendulum is swinging the opposite way. Some Christians now seem to minimize the importance of physical structures, as if buildings don't matter at all.

Of course the Church is not a building. It's people. *Living stones.*

But as I go abroad, I've seen that buildings really are important. I am convinced that in His eternal scheme of things, God cares about bricks and concrete.

Mortar matters.

The Relentless Friend

The real hero of the story of the leper church is the young man who took us there the first time. If he had not been so incredibly persistent, we never would have gone. After all, we were busy doing good things; it would have been easy to turn him down. But he was relentless on behalf of his friends, and if we had not gone, what would have happened to Deborah? Would the people's beloved church ever have been completed? We don't know. All we know is that because of that young man, God used us to make a difference.

He's like the men in the New Testament who brought their paralyzed friend to Jesus. They couldn't get him in the front door of the house where Jesus was teaching. The crowds would not make way. They did not give up. Next thing Jesus knew, pieces of plaster and tile, or whatever made ceilings in those days, were crashing all around Him, and here came the paralyzed man, his eyes real big, lowered right before Jesus by his grinning friends. The Bible says Jesus saw their faith and said to the sick boy, "Son, your sins are forgiven." Incredible.

It reminds me of a friend of ours who got involved in prison ministry. Tom, an entrepreneur who owns a large business, was on the board at his children's school, a deacon in his church, and had no time in his schedule to spare. Then a friend of a friend of his teenaged daughter drifted into drugs and crime. The boy ended up in prison.

Tom didn't hear about it for a long time. When he did, he prayed for the young man. Then one of the teenagers called him. "Mr. Miller," he said hesitantly, "we're, uh, wondering if you'd go visit Jack in prison." Tom sympathized but was able to put off the teenager without much trouble.

The next evening he found a note in his mailbox, urging him to reconsider.

The night after that, a car pulled into his driveway and the doorbell rang. Tom groaned when he looked through the window and saw the teenager. The message was the same: "Mr. Miller, I don't mean to, like, bug you, but Jack really needs somebody."

You know what happened. Bugged into action, Tom went to see Jack in prison. Jack accepted Christ. Tom couldn't just leave him hanging, so he started going to the institution once a week for a Bible study. Other inmates started coming, and next thing Tom knew, he had been going to that prison once a week for six years—God's instrument of change for the lives of many, many prisoners.

Sometimes, like Tom, we're the person who's being bugged. When that happens, we had better give up our precious time and do what God would have us do. And sometimes, like that teenager and that young Indian man and the friends of the paralytic, we need to be relentless in the quest to bring help to those whom God loves.

Mortar Matters

Dois

For years, I didn't have a particular interest in building churches. Sure, I'd contribute whenever my home church had a building campaign, and since I had real estate businesses, I always noticed architecture and aesthetics and steeples and such. But building buildings was not a hot button for me.

Then, on my first trip to India, I saw what an enormous difference a church building could make in a given community. The reality of the spiritual battle at hand was very clear. I felt compelled to do what I could to help.

Ellen

I had not been to India before I went there with Dois. Just to keep it interesting, he arranged our trip during the biggest Hindu festival in the history of the world, a full moon, and a massive earthquake that shook the entire subcontinent and killed more than 50,000 people.

It was late January. As the fat moon rose over India, the astronomical positions of Jupiter and the constellations Aquarius and Aries heralded the climax of the Maha Kumbh Mela—when millions of Hindu pilgrims converged on the city of Allahabad, believing that a ritual bath in the waters of the Ganges River would purge them and guarantee salvation.

129

We were in Calcutta at the time and opened a newspaper to see large photos of naked pilgrims carrying ceremonial tridents, their faces smeared with ash. It looked like Woodstock revisited, Indian-style: hordes of pilgrims smoking hemp and dipping in the Ganges–a river that in fact flows with raw sewage, the remains of partially cremated human bodies, and animal carcasses.

But it was the newspaper headline that shook us most: "Freed From Sins," it proclaimed. It was like seeing Old Testament idol worship come alive. Here were millions of human beings desperately seeking deliverance–to the point that they hoped filthy water might wash away their sins.

Perhaps for many Indians the Ganges bath was simply a cultural celebration. But for many, it represented a sincere spiritual search–that insatiable human hunger for forgiveness that can come only through divine sacrifice.

Sacrifice

In some places in the world, sacrifice is more literal than Americans can understand.

If you ride many miles over bumpy roads to a remote rock outcropping in the eastern part of India, you will come to a small, bright church. It is the center of the rural community, and spiritual home to about 140 men, women, and children.

Just a few years ago, there were no Christians in this rocky valley. Villagers followed a multitude of Hindu gods, routinely giving offerings of rice, rupees, or fruit, and when the circumstances warranted, some went even further.

Near the village is an immense natural formation of large rocks. Some stand vertically on end in a hollow around a horizontal shelf-like stone. Years ago a desperate man was out of his mind with despair over his wife's grave illness. He carried his small child to the stone altar, a heavy hatchet in his hand. He pleaded with the Hindu gods. "Heal my wife," he prayed. And then he swung his axe, beheading his child. Blood flowed over the edge of long, smooth stone.

Eventually believers from another part of India traveled to that village. They visited from hut to hut. They brought a medical team to care for the villagers who were suffering from malaria. They started a Bible study, teaching the people about Jesus from the Gospel of John. Gradually, people decided to trust the God who did not demand human sacrifice but instead came to earth to sacrifice Himself for human sin.

The new Christians were so excited about this great news that they shared their faith with others. A pastor was eventually sent to shepherd the growing band of believers. We contracted with them to build a sanctuary, and today, that little church in the valley rings with praises to God as the people there reach out to the people of the surrounding countryside.

That small church is a picture of the power that can change our world.

To some, it might seem insignificant. It's great to build a   village church, of course, but of what strategic relevance is a remote outpost of 140 Christians in a nation of a billion human beings?

Humanly speaking, it's not strategic at all.

But divine strategies work in the face of the impossible.

After all, Jesus left the entire plan for His Church, the continuation of His ministry, in the hands of eleven flawed disciples who had already proved themselves lacking in follow-through. Not much of a strategic plan.

Those first believers went on to tell the Gospel. Churches grew, multiplied, and were scattered abroad, continually reproducing themselves.

Making Disciples

Twenty-one centuries later, the vitality of the church goes on, one changed life at a time. Now we use technology to transmit the Good News as far and wide as possible so that evangelistic outreaches via television, radio, the Internet, or other means can serve as catalysts for spiritual transformation.

But the means for the ongoing process of sanctification will always be the local church. For it is there that the work of *discipleship* is done.

Generally speaking, evangelism without discipleship does not go deep enough to root and nurture believers in Christian maturity. For example, consider the explosion of new believers in Africa in the late 1980s. At that time the Lausanne Committee on Evangelism, on whose advisory board I served, estimated that 16,000 people were coming to faith in Christ every day. The seed of the Gospel was going out in great quantities, and people were receiving it eagerly.

But within a few years, many of those who had embraced Christianity had fallen away, seduced by cults. They had not been discipled in the context of a healthy local church. Unshepherded and unaccountable, they were unable to discern truth from error and fell prey to false teachings.

Please hear what I am saying: *Evangelism is absolutely crucial.* We must spread the Good News however we can. But we must also provide the means for new believers to be nurtured in their faith, so they might withstand the storms of temptation and false teaching that will surely come their way.

The greenhouse for healthy spiritual growth is the local church, led by equipped leaders who can teach the Word of Truth. We have developed training centers as well as churches, so lay leaders can be theologically trained. The key to deep-rooted, stable growth is foundational preaching of the Word of God.

That's why I get excited about building churches, not just planting congregations. Our brothers and sisters in poor countries abroad need sanctuaries, physical temples, where the people of God can gather, worship Him, celebrate the sacraments, and digest the red meat of the Word. As we've seen, by gathering in a physical place, they demonstrate what the Kingdom of God is all about, and others in the community are drawn to faith.

Objections

Some people have let me know they don't share my enthusiasm for funding bricks and mortar abroad. As far as I can tell, such opposition falls into one of two categories. First:

Why get involved in foreign building projects when there are needs here at home?

The leader of a Protestant denomination once said to me, "If the people in those countries want a church, let them build it!"

The beauty of the Body at work is that God calls each individual part to function as He wants us to, so that as a corporate organism we might reach out to *every* arena of human need. Some are called to give and work within the U.S., in inner cities, among high school or university students, among the sick, the elderly, those in prison. I salute those who are called to those arenas of need in our country. My work abroad has never meant I've discontinued my support of such ministries.

But I do believe God gives each of us a central calling–and He equips us to fulfill that calling.

For me, the calling is to help the Church in the Third World. Believers in Cuba or Congo or Cambodia, for example, cannot afford to build houses of worship. Our U.S. dollars go so far to provide for them what they cannot provide for themselves.

Here's the second objection I encounter:

Why bother with buildings? Why not just build up the Body of Christ?

I think those questions come from a false division between the sacred and the secular. As I've mentioned, I used to think that way as well. On one side was the material world, and on the other, the things of the Spirit. The things of the world were visible, the things of God invisible.

But God owns it all. He doesn't look down on "stuff"–He uses material things as tools for His eternal purposes. The physical building is a tool to build up the people–the spiritual Body of Christ.

The Old Testament accounts of the building of the Tabernacle and the Temple are full of God's specific directions about architecture, fabrics, colors, decorations, aromas–through these physical means human beings would be drawn to worship Him.

God no longer dwells in a Tabernacle; He lives in human hearts. But He is still Lord over all creation. Just as the world around us declares His glory, so can the works of our hands. Whether it's the magnificent stained glass of a great cathedral or the simple cross atop a country church, these physical things incline our hearts toward the spiritual realities they represent.

Objectives

So far we haven't built any cathedrals. The churches we build in Indian villages are basic structures, which seat about two hundred people. Either they are constructed of handmade, sundried brick or, in many areas, a kind of mineral block.

The local believers invest sweat equity into their church building. They mix the mortar by hand. Then a mason stacks the blocks and cements them together. Gradually, the walls go up, and the workers put the roof on, usually a four-inch concrete roof. We try to build strong buildings that will last for many years. At the end, we lay a concrete floor.

In China, the process is similar. I recall the pastor in Hunan province who was building her church. When we came to visit, she greeted us in rubber boots, her hands covered with concrete dust. In the congregation were men who had served prison terms for their faith during Mao Zedong's Cultural Revolution. Now they were pouring cement. The older women worked right with them. Some grinned, pointed toward the sky, and showed me the buttons they wore on their chests—pictures of Jesus, in a land where Chairman Mao's photo is posted everywhere except in the hearts of believers.

Miracle in Gujarat

In some parts of the world, building churches is not just a physical challenge, but a spiritual one. In the Gujarat state of India, militant Hindus set themselves against 40 congregations in a mountainous area where the Christian community had grown by 400 percent in the last few years, with new churches built all over the countryside.

Backed by fanatical sources, Hindu activists came to the area to intimidate Christians and halt the growth of the church however they could. They had the local pastors' names. They knew where they lived. They knew where their children went to school.

Four of the pastors were attacked, beaten, and released. They didn't know what would come next...but then the news came that an enormous Hindu rally was to be held in the heart of the Christian community. A new shrine was built; new roads leading to it were paved, and a dam built to create a lake where Christians would be forced to be re-baptized.

The believers learned that the Hindus had called for 500,000 people to come to the rally for the purpose of identifying Christians and forcing them to become Hindus. Hindu leaders went to each home in the area and asked if the occupants were Hindus. If the people said they were, then a flag was put up in front of the house. If the answer was no, then they were told to denounce their faith in Christ and embrace Hinduism. If the Christians refused, the leader would pronounce a curse on the family and leave, with no flag in front of the house.

To those of us in the U.S., this situation sounded like a scene from the Old Testament. We joined together with Christians all over India earnestly praying for our brothers and sisters in Gujarat. The local pastors came together–including those who had been beaten by the militants–crying out to God to work in their midst.

The hours went by. In the U.S. we didn't hear anything for several days after the Hindu rally. Then, finally, an anti-climactic email arrived from our partner in Gujarat, saying simply that the Hindu rally had been an absolute flop, and that no Christians had been forced to be re-baptized as Hindus. God had intervened!

Miracles in Africa

In Congo, we visited a group of believers in an area called Manenga. Their pastor and his wife lived in a shack about a mile off the main, dusty road. Early every Sunday morning they would take all their furniture out so the congregation would have a place to worship; late every Sunday night they'd move it all back.

As these people started to build their church, they had to carry all of the construction materials to the site by hand. But they persisted and over time built a small, neat church. On dedication day it was crammed with people from the village, singing and worshiping God as only Africans can. And now the children of that village, which formerly had no school, meet in the church building for their education.

In a church in Zimbabwe, a woman from the community was diagnosed with AIDS, the scourge that is killing millions of Africans. She called for the elders of the Mufakose Church to pray for her. They did so, following the biblical guidelines in the Epistle of James. When doctors checked her condition again, they found no trace of AIDS or HIV. The woman returned to the village and told everyone who would listen what God had done for her. As a result, most of the villagers committed themselves to Jesus. At first, they had no place to worship, so they would gather under a large tree.

After we helped them build a church, we returned for its dedication. There was no electricity, but lanterns swayed in the breeze, giving a soft glow to the hundreds of faces gathered to worship God. Later one of the leaders told me, "People here think of Christianity as a western religion. But when they have a church building in their own village, then Christianity becomes part of their culture."

Do bricks and mortar make a difference? I think they do.

In Ukraine, the churches we build are more expensive, since they must have heat for the long, dark winters. There they cost, on average, $25,000. Though simple in construction, each is a work of art.

I remember visiting one church that was almost completed. Its people were not expecting us. The women were outside, mixing plaster. They brought us inside and pointed up to the ceiling. A local artist–a sort of Ukrainian Michelangelo–had lain on his back on a flimsy scaffold and painted an incredible scene. Against a pale blue background I could see mighty angels and golden clouds around an ascending Christ. Its beauty took my breath away.

In another Ukrainian church, the local mayor came to the dedication service. Though not a Christian, as he listened to the Word of God and gazed at the hand-painted murals, he began to weep. "I never cry," he told the pastor. "But I can't help it. Here I sense God. This is a place where people can find His peace."

Of course, the beautiful thing about these churches in Ukraine is the absolute luxury of building them; after all, church building was banned in the old Soviet Union. In many villages, we're helping to build the first new churches in more than seventy years.

Bricks to the Glory of God

In one such case, the government granted a group of believers a swampland for church construction. It took six months, but the Christians packed the marshy bog with fill dirt–wheelbarrow by wheelbarrow. Once they had prepared the site, they could not obtain any bricks to construct their building, so local officials permitted them to tear down a nearby unused nuclear missile silo, a relic of the Cold War.

When the believers started dismantling the silo and carrying the bricks away–again, wheelbarrow by wheelbarrow–one man found a fragile slip of paper, rolled tightly and stuck between two bricks. The others gathered around as he carefully unrolled the old paper and smoothed it flat.

"These bricks," he read out loud, straining to decipher the faded ink, "were purchased to build a house of worship. But they were confiscated by the government to build a missile silo. May it please the Lord that these bricks will one day be used to build a house to His glory!"

And so they were.

The Church as Community Center

When we build churches abroad, particularly in small villages, they become the focal point of the community.

That was once the case in the United States. In early New England each town had its village green, at the center of which was the church with its white steeple and its graveyard where ancestors lay in the stony sod. The church was the center of social, intellectual, and spiritual life. All of life was connected, with none of the compartmentalization that modern secularism has brought to American life.

As the influence of real Christianity waned, the church was no longer the center of community life. It was replaced by city hall, the shopping mall, and the sports arena.

But in countless communities in less wealthy countries, the little churches we build become the center of community life.

Take India. Because of the difficult religious climate there, we do not always call the churches we build "churches," even though they have a cross on top and are clearly places of worship. In many cases, we receive permits to build "community centers."

Not only do believers worship and fellowship there, but the buildings are also open to the community and Christians take care to provide all kinds of helpful social services.

Drawing Others In

For example, in a country where more than half the population cannot read, literacy training is a great ministry. Many of the churches we build also serve as classrooms for teaching adults and children to read their own language. (Often, the study text happens to be the Gospel of John.)

Many village women have no marketable skills. So churches like the Madhapuram congregation offer sewing instruction. Believers constructed a little outbuilding outfitted with old treadle Singer sewing machines. Several of the church women teach classes for villagers, free of charge.

Medical services are also a great help. Trained physicians travel from village to village on a monthly rotation. People can come to the community center and have illnesses diagnosed and treated; they also learn basic hygiene and health skills that we in the West take for granted.

You have to remember that I'm talking about remote parts of India, where witch doctors are still the usual recourse. Many villagers pay dearly only to have the local witch doctor slaughter a chicken, perform a dubious ritual involving its entrails, and fail to cure their ills. The physical care, as well as the attention and tenderness the medical staff provides, opens villagers' hearts further to the love of the Great Physician.

Keeping Up with the Christians

The other great thing that happens is that the church sets a new standard in the village. You've heard of the "broken windows" theory in New York City. A few years ago officials there discovered that when they left broken windows or graffiti in a ghetto area, the breakage and defacement continued at an even faster rate. When no care was taken, people took that as a message that no care was needed.

But when officials cleaned up a wall or fixed a window immediately after the damage, it stayed clean and whole. Residents got a taste of civic pride. They saw that their community was worth keeping up—and they did their part to continue that trend.

The same principle applies around the world. I can't tell you how many times we've constructed a clean, new church, the only masonry building in the area. Then the villagers begin to take more pride in their own homes. They build permanent houses rather than huts. Then, before you know it, the government comes in and digs a well. Remember the little leper colony church we told you about earlier? After it was completed, local officials actually built new housing for the men and women in that ostracized village.

The church-as-community center accomplishes several good things. First, it gives a sense of identity for the local Body of Christ, a place where believers can gather and worship Him. Second, in serving the needs of the local people, it draws many to a relationship with Christ. And third, it raises the bar in the community, setting a new standard of excellence there.

Sanctuary

Believers in China face strict mandates about proselytizing. In many provinces, they cannot tell people in the market or even on the road right in front of their church about their faith. Such talk is forbidden on the street.

But within the four walls of their government-approved church, they can worship and speak freely about Jesus. One congregation built a fellowship hall next to their sanctuary, which is open to the neighborhood, for people to come in for a snack, read, or relax on a quiet sofa for conversation—which just might turn out to be about the love of God.

In Vietnam, the atmosphere is much the same. Once one of our donors returned from a trip there and told us that in addition to giving money to build a large church, he also wanted to pay to have air-conditioning put in. Our usual practice is to fund the building but not to provide items like sound systems, pews, air-conditioning, or other "extras."

But this donor insisted. When we asked him why this 2,000-member church needed an air-conditioning system, his answer surprised us. While Vietnam's climate is very hot, humid, and oppressive, constant government surveillance proves to be even more oppressive. As in China, church members are not allowed to preach or evangelize on the street, but if they are on church property, they may do so.

Our donor friend likened air-conditioning to the use of electricity during the great tent revivals in the U.S. at the end of the nineteenth century. People would come from miles around to see light bulbs at work—and in the meantime, they would hear the Gospel. Many were converted. They saw the Light when all they had come to see was a light bulb.

In the same way, few public buildings in Vietnam are air-conditioned. After that cool church was built, people sought relief from the heat of the streets, and many came to Christ.

One final picture of how mortar–or in this case, two pieces of wood–matters.

When we visited a remote area in the mountains of southern China, we traveled for eight hours to the San Fang church. The foundation was laid, and the walls were going up. The building was situated high on a ridge between two narrow streets. It was hard to transport construction materials up there, and I wondered why the local people had chosen an area so difficult to access.

But as we departed, I saw why. As we made our way back down toward the city, the narrow mountain road looped back on itself many times. At each switchback, I looked up and saw, many kilometers in the distance, the half-finished San Fang church, its brick walls rising up on that high, faraway ridge. And so, when that church was completed, the most visible sight for miles around in that part of China was the soaring sign of Christ's cross.

Sanctuary

In the U.S. we haven't experienced the kinds of restrictions that our fellow Christians in communist countries have. We're free to talk about Christ on the street and in most public places. But the notion of sanctuary–a safe, welcoming place to shelter people from life's storms–is universal. Not just in our churches but in our homes. Our attention to physical details there can make them spiritual havens. In our often-cold culture, Christians can practice radical hospitality just by opening our homes.

Anne lives in a neighborhood of upper-middle class families. Anne and her husband have several children; they both work full-time, though Anne is a writer and works from home. They are comfortable but have less than their neighbors, many of whom employ fulltime nannies, interior designers, maids, lawn services, you name it.

One neighbor had all that and more. She was always just coming from a manicure, a pedicure, a facial, the spa. She catered perfect dinner parties during which the nanny watched the children; the caterers stayed to clean up afterward.

Sometimes Anne struggled with jealousy. Her toenails were unpainted. She cleaned her own toilets. Her dinner parties were often spontaneous and usually consisted of burgers on the grill and paper plates. Lacking a staff, she made her children drape white towels over their little arms and serve the appetizers. Her husband was grill-meister. But there was laughter and music, a large, furry dog, and the love of God overflowing for all.

Anne knew that brittle perfection is not all it's cracked up to be. Her neighbor's husband was gone most of the time, working obsessively to fund their trophy life. Their quest for the perfect lifestyle seemed slightly manic, hollow of real living.

In the end, the neighbor started spending more and more time, not in her own magazine-perfect house, but in Anne's home. Her children came too, without the nanny. They laughed and ate off paper plates and learned to pray. Anne could see her neighbor warming up, letting down, breathing deep, sinking her roots into a place called home.

Sanctuary.

Weaving the Real Worldwide Web
Dois

Though it is in the eastern part of the country, the state of Bihar is the Wild West of India. Tour books warn travelers about its political instability and random law enforcement, and it has long been home to fanatical groups who hate the Gospel.

So over the years, Christian missionaries made a point to go to Bihar. Many were martyred. So many, in fact, that Bihar has been called "the graveyard of missionaries."

But the Church is alive in Bihar.

An Indian pastor named N. J. Varughese is hard at work there. About ten years ago, N. J. was preaching in an open market. He saw seven or eight men standing to the side of the crowd. Their hair was long and wild. They were crusted with dirt. A few scraps of ragged cloth covered their loins. And they were   listening intently to everything that N. J. said.

After his message he approached the men and recognized that they were "monkey people"–members of a primitive, nomadic tribe who live in jungle areas and eat monkey meat. They were considered the lowest of the low by other cultural groups in India.

"Why are you here?" N. J. asked. Though he couldn't speak their dialect, he could communicate with them well enough in Hindi.

"We like your singing!" they told him. And as they talked a while longer, they invited N. J. to come to their village the next day. "We want to hear more about your God," they said.

The next day, N. J. and his evangelistic team traveled deep into a remote part of Bihar and found the encampment. The monkey people had cut long, slender tree branches, bent them in a graceful semicircle between two stakes, and decorated the welcoming arch with flowers. They had laid colorful mats on the ground for the missionaries to sit on.

N. J. and the others sang gospel songs, shared Bible stories, and told the people about the God who hung on the cross. Then, as the afternoon passed into evening and darkness fell, the team brought out a generator, a few light bulbs, and a slide show about the life of Christ.

At the sight of the electric bulb, the people stared in absolute amazement. "What is that?" the adults and children cried out together.

"It's the light," N. J. told them, grinning because his words were more true than they guessed. "The Light has come to your village!"

Many of the monkey people put their faith in Jesus that evening, and within a few months, almost all the members of that community had become Christians. Before this, they had worshiped trees and sacrificed chickens and goats to jungle spirits.

Now, by the power of the Holy Spirit, they were falling in love with Jesus. They began having "church" every morning at five o'clock before going out to hunt monkeys. One of N. J.'s colleagues, Satish, taught them more about the Scriptures, how to pray and how to grow deeper in their faith even though they could not read or write.

Sometime later, a group of the monkey people traveled to Orissa. They sang gospel songs in a marketplace, where a group of curious onlookers surrounded them.

"What are you doing? Why are you so happy?" they were asked.

The monkey people didn't mince words.

"We found God!" said one. "His name is Jesus. He changed our lives. We don't lie or steal or hurt anyone anymore. We don't know much... but He changed us and forgave our sins! If you want to know more, go to our pastor, and he will tell you!"

"Where is the pastor?" asked the people.

"In Ranchi," came the response.

The town of Ranchi was a hundred miles away, but those people from the market walked that distance, camping along the way. When they arrived in the tribal area, Pastor Satish shared the Gospel with them, and the market people gave their lives to Christ. They lived among the monkey people for a while, learning more about Jesus, and then went back to Orissa.

Today, as a result of *their* witness, there is a church of 350 believers there.

Meanwhile the faith of the monkey people keeps multiplying... about a thousand members of the tribe have received Christ, and their lives have changed dramatically. Their children now go to school. Adults are learning to read. They have learned how to raise vegetables and irrigate land. They've dug wells and bought tractors; some have bank accounts. Some have built permanent houses. A few have even gone together to start a fish farm.

They all keep fishing for men and women. They've planted seven churches. They have about fifteen full-time Christian workers who continue to spread the seed of evangelism and then disciple new believers.

Because of the dramatic change in the monkey people, many other people have turned to Christ. They've encountered hostility from militant Hindus. Some have been put in jail; many have been beaten up.

But in their usual plainspoken way, the monkey men say this: "All we know is that we used to cheat, we used to lie . . . no *religion* changed our lives. Only a *Person:* Only Jesus Christ!"

Now, the monkey people offer a fairly exotic example–you just don't see many members of the monkey tribe on the streets of suburbia. But I love their story because it illustrates the basic principles of how God builds His Church.

The Gospel goes out.
People respond.
New believers are discipled.
They tell others.
The group of Christians grows.
They build a church in which to worship.
The process starts over, and perpetuates itself–over and over again.

The Resilient Strength of the Kingdom

That reproducing model is not rocket science. It is the way God has perpetuated His Church since its beginnings. We're just trying to get on board with how He works. We do use a new term for His pattern though. We call it the *web effect.*

Since the explosion of the Internet, the metaphor of a worldwide web has become a great mental picture of the communications connections that can link people all over the world. But I like to think that facilitating the growth of churches around the planet is spinning the *real* worldwide web.

When a spider spins a web, its silk is made up of chains of amino acids. Spider silk is about five times stronger than steel and twice as strong as Kevlar of the same weight. (Kevlar is the material used to make bulletproof vests.) Arachnologists say that a single strand of spider silk, thick as a pencil, could stop a 747 in flight. For its weight, it is the toughest material on the planet.

Yet it is also incredibly elastic, able to stretch to thirty percent longer than its original length without breaking.

The strength and resiliency of the spider's physical web is a tremendous reminder to me of the spiritual power and flexibility God gives His spiritual webs. If God can so equip a lowly spider– just as He looks after the lilies of the field–how much more will He equip the webbing growth of His Church?

The web effect will manifest itself differently in different cultures and conditions. As I write right now, we have hundreds of churches under construction in various parts of the world. Our extraordinary finance department is wildly wiring American dollars to foreign banks that turn them into everything from pesos to rupees to rubles. Our communications team works feverishly to send updates to donors all over the U.S. regarding the churches they're funding.

The Mini Bible College department currently handles 27 languages with more on the way. We're at work in countries where Christians are a tiny minority, in places where communist officials scrutinize the ministry for any possible infraction, nations whose bureaucracies are mind-boggling, and in African republics where the governments seem to change every few months.

Given all these factors—and many, many more—the growth of each new congregation is different. Building each new sanctuary is different. What we're doing is humanly impossible. *But God keeps doing the impossible,* and new churches are being completed and dedicated to His glory every month.

This means that the webbing concept works, but it is not a set of policies and procedures, nor is it a product of North American culture. We have just seen how God builds His Church and then aligns the ministry with *His* way of doing things.

Sowing Seeds, Reaping Souls

In the Gospels Jesus talks about the farmer sowing the seed of the Word of God. The farmer of the parable uses the hand-sowing method common in his day, in which large areas were spread generously with seed so that some—though not all—would take root and grow. Another name for that seeding technique is still in use today: broadcasting. Even those of us who aren't farmers probably have a broadcast spreader in our garages to use when we fertilize our lawns.

Radio and the Internet use the same technique. With them, the Gospel seed is spread liberally to millions and billions of people.

As in Jesus' parable, some will not respond. Others will receive it gladly and multiply a hundred fold.

George of the Jungle

One of our first experiences with radio in India was with a man we call George. That's not his name, of course. That's just what we call him. George was the leader of his village in southeastern India. He began listening to the Mini Bible College radio broadcast each day; he had never heard such things. Since there was no church in his village and he had never traveled much beyond it, he wrote a simple letter to the address given on the broadcast. He received a Bible in Telegu. George committed his life to Christ. His family saw the change in his life; they prayed to receive Jesus as well.

When we first visited George years ago, we arrived early on a Sunday morning. Beaming, he welcomed us into his home, a small hut with vines and juniper branches hanging from the roof. Breezes blew through the open windows. George's family, dressed in their best, shyly welcomed us. His wife served cups of steaming tea.

The neighbors got wind of our visit. Soon George's little house was packed with villagers, with dozens more standing in the doorway, hanging in the windows, and gathered in the lane outside.

George showed us the Mini Bible College notes he had received from writing into the radio station. He read from his well-worn Bible. We prayed together and sang a few gospel songs. But our voices were few in the midst of the crowd that had gathered, and we realized there was no way we could leave that place until we preached the Word.

Burt Reed opened his Bible and told the people about the love of God. After that, we all knelt in prayer on George's dirt floor. With tears coursing down his face, one of the Indian brothers with us whispered, "This is the first worship service ever held in this village."

From that first service, a group of believers grew. George was their leader. But he needed training. As we became aware of the needs of new congregations like George's, we realized that the new churches that were sprouting would need new pastors.

Some came from denominations already at work in the country. But God also opened doors for us to join with national partners to build pastoral training centers where students could receive solid biblical teaching as well as field experience with established mentors.

As I write, these centers have graduated about eight hundred trained pastors and missionaries–including the young man who arrived at the training center in Hyderabad after having walked from Myanmar (Burma)–a month-long trek. Today he and others like him are leading churches in the eastern part of India and even venturing into villages located in Nepal, Bhutan, and Bangladesh to share the Gospel.[3]

The Thursday morning men's Bible study group near my home–still meeting after all these years–gave funds to build the Hyderabad training center, joining with the Williamsburg Community Chapel. The guys wanted to call it the Dick Woodward Training Center. But Dick would have none of it. "Don't you dare name it after me," he said. "Give glory to God."

George of the jungle eventually attended the "training-center-not-named-after-Dick-Woodward," which graduates about thirty students every year. After completing his studies, George pastored the church in his village and today is a church-planter in an area 150 kilometers away from his home village.

One more thing.

George's Madapuram church, which began with that tea party and spontaneous worship service years ago, had at last count planted 400 congregations in India. We even have a diagram of it on paper–the mother church, with all those daughters springing out, which in turn have created more and more offshoots. It looks an awful lot like a beautiful spiderweb. With more like it, we could web all of India.

Pay It Forward
Dois

Some years ago a charitable movement made its way across the western United States. People gave luxury cars to strangers, forgave one another terrible wrongs, gave money to people in need. One person even died in someone else's place.

Of course, these wonderful things took place not in real life but in the film *Pay It Forward*. The movie is about an eleven-year-old boy named Trevor, a poor kid who lives in Las Vegas with his single, alcoholic mother.

On the first day of school, Trevor's social studies teacher gives the class an assignment: Come up with one idea that can make the world a better place and then put it into action.

Trevor's idea is called "pay it forward." The rules are simple: Do "something big" for three people, and then, instead of having them return the kindness, tell them to do the same for three other people. That is, pay it forward.

By "something big," Trevor means something that the person can't do for himself. And it must involve some sacrifice, so as to create a sense of gratitude and obligation. But the recipient doesn't pay back the giver—instead, he or she returns the favor to someone new, who, in turn, passes it on.

What a great idea!

Moral people of various faiths–or of no apparent spiritual commitment–can and do pay it forward. Helping others is part of America's heritage. It's rooted in a shared set of moral assumptions about sacrifice, self-denial, and the common good. Good citizens, Christian and non-Christian, do unassuming works of service among those who cannot pay them back.

But the idea's greatest power comes in a Christian context.

Amazing Grace

First, helping someone who cannot pay you back is an *act of grace*. Its unmerited favor reflects God's grace. Christ died in our place and gives us life that lasts forever. We don't deserve it. We can't earn it. We can never pay Him back.

So we don't do good things as a way of deserving our salvation. We do good because we have freely received God's good grace. Lavishly grateful, we seek to do what pleases Him. We love God and others as a response to what *He* has initiated: "We love because he first loved us" (1 John 4:19).

Second, it's easy to pay it forward when we see ourselves as *stewards*. If everything belongs to God, then I don't own anything. So of course I need not be "paid back." It all belongs to Him.

Third, in its fullest sense, paying it forward has to be seen in the scope of *eternity*. The good we do for others is not just part of a random daisy chain here on earth. There is an overarching Designer at work, an omniscient, sovereign God who uses human actions here and now for His indescribable eternal plan.

God is unleashing an incredibly powerful chain reaction that can change nations, a catalyst that can leap across continents. The Holy Spirit is working in the world today through an extraordinary network of exponential causes and effects, connections and links that make the Internet look like child's play. God is on the move through His people all over the world, and He cannot be stopped.

I tell you this–imperfectly, I know–to try to give a sense of the big-picture vision that fuels my excitement about what God is doing today. In what we've described to you so far, I hope you've seen the intrinsic *multiplying* effect as we build churches that build up the people, the Body of Christ. As God's Spirit spins His worldwide web, the Gospel goes on ... and on ... and on.

When we celebrated the start of construction of our two thousandth church, for example, it was a wonderful day. But because each church contracts to plant at least five more, we weren't celebrating just our two thousandth church, but in time, our ten thousandth church. At the very least.

And each of our partners working around the world is part of the equation by which God is building His Church. As these gifted friends concentrate on their areas–their franchises, if you will–they are collectively advancing the Kingdom through the building of churches, the nurturing of congregations, and the building of training centers.

The equation is laid out to perpetuate itself until Christ returns. It is not something we made up. It's the intrinsic nature of the Church itself.

Greater Things

Jesus started the chain reaction at the Last Supper. "I tell you the truth," He said to His followers, "anyone who has faith in me will do what I have been doing."

Eyebrows went up. The disciples had seen Jesus cast out demons, heal the chronically ill, raise the dead. How were they going to do all that?

But then Jesus went further. "He will do even greater things than these, because I am going to the Father."

"Greater things?"

In His earthly ministry, Jesus was confined to one body. Part of the limitation He took on in His incarnation was that He be present in one place at one time. So His works were done one at a time, so to speak.

After Pentecost, Christ's disciples proclaimed the Good News. They baptized new believers, gathered them into communities, and the Church began to grow. As the decades and centuries rolled out, thousands, then millions, of people came to faith.

Gifted in a thousand different ways and powered by the one same Holy Spirit, they invaded every arena of human life.[4]

It's incredible. After Christ's ascension, His Spirit descended to empower His Body–His people–to do more than He could accomplish as one person here on earth. So even as you read this paragraph, believers in Mongolia, Brazil, Bangladesh, Peoria, and ten thousand other places are advancing Christ's Kingdom. We are not in this alone. We are part of something far more magnificent and huge than we can begin to imagine.

And it's far too big for us to track.

Sure, each of us should assess our stewardship and strive to make sure that our ministry is as excellent, lean, and productive as possible.

But we cannot measure what God is doing. We don't know the extent by which God is multiplying, building, extending His Kingdom. And it's good we don't know–otherwise, as human beings, we might get caught up in numbers. We might try to quantify, and sometimes even take credit, for His work.

Immeasurable

As my friend Lee Earl has put it, when Jesus was on this earth, He could be measured. You could measure how tall He was, how big His feet were, His hat size. Then "one day Jesus went airborne–He went from being something measurable to something immeasurable." It's only in eternity that we will have any sure sense of what He is doing through us down here.

Lee says, "We have to become comfortable with what we can know and what we can measure, in terms of ministry results and accountability, . . . and we have to become comfortable with what we don't know and cannot measure."

Too much focus on measurements and numbers can also tempt us toward "if, then" formulas regarding God's will: If we do X, then He'll do Y. If we give $100, then He'll bring 11.25 souls to Himself. If some tragedy occurs, then we'll soon see how God caused "all things to work together for good" because of it.

But God is God–too big for our formulas, His purposes too high to be boxed by our limited human perspective.

God Is God

As Dick Woodward says, "I know God could heal me if He wanted to. But He has chosen not to. But it's okay. Why? *Because God is God.*"

Elisabeth Elliott has said the same thing. Reflecting on the murders of her husband and four other missionaries at the hands of the Auca tribesmen (now known as the Waorani), she writes that the story . . .

> pointed to one thing: *God is God.* If He is God, He is worthy of my worship and my service. I will find rest nowhere but in His will, and that will is infinitely, immeasurably, unspeakably beyond my largest notions of what He is up to . . . .
>
> There is always the urge to oversimplify, to weigh in at once with interpretations that cannot possibly cover all the data or stand up to close inspection. We know, for example, that time and again in the history of the Christian church, the blood of martyrs has been its seed. We are tempted to assume a simple equation here. Five men died. This will mean X-number of Waorani Christians.
>
> Perhaps so. Perhaps not. Cause and effect are in God's hands. Is it not the part of faith simply to let them rest there? *God is God.*"[1]

So, even as we celebrate the idea of paying it forward, knowing that God multiplies our ministry investments, we take care not to think in formulas. Sometimes He allows us to see an incredible harvest of souls. Sometimes He does not.

But one thing we know: Christ paid it forward at Calvary. That sacrifice changed history. He is on the move. He *is* building His Church today, and it's advancing steadily on those doomed gates of hell.

And the wild truth is this: *I* can be part of changing the world. So can you. Pay it forward to someone today in some small way–and the adventures will begin.

[1][Elisabeth Elliott, *Through Gates of Splendor,* Revised Edition, 1986 (Tyndale House Publishers, Carol Stream, IL) 267 - 68].

"Let the Little Children Come to Me"
Dois

One of the clearest examples of paying it forward is investing in the next generation. As we build churches around the world, the most dramatic evidence of their impact is the way the lives of children are changed for good, as in those church-orphanages in Cambodia that save children from starvation and prostitution.

In Ukraine, as church growth explodes in that formerly communist nation, believers are reaching out to children via street ministry, Gospel-based puppet shows, and Bible clubs. Victor Kulbich, our irrepressible Ukrainian partner, says, "We use every tool available for evangelism, but none grows the church more than children's ministries."

Clearly. At one Kiev church, 12,000 children came to Christ in one year through the church's puppet ministry, and those children, in turn, brought *thirty percent* of the adults who became Christians in the church that same year.

Another congregation was given a former kindergarten building to be used as a Christian school. Under communist rule, kindergarten was the beginning of official indoctrination in the state religion of atheism. Now, as soon as it's rehabbed, that same facility will be a place whose halls echo with the name of Jesus.

In Congo a few years ago, I was visiting a church school we had helped to build. I noticed a little girl using a stick to draw in the sand. She was about eight years old, and a bunch of kids were gathered around her. As I drew closer, I saw she was tracing out math equations. I found out that it costs two dollars a week to attend the Christian school. The rest of the kids just didn't have that kind of money. So that little girl would go to school in the morning, then gather the kids together in the afternoon and teach them what she had learned. Needless to say, we provided scholarships for the rest of those children.

A New Name

We don't even know what to say about some of the children God helps.

In early 2002, Randy, an American traveling with us, was entertaining the children in one of our Cambodian orphanages. A ventriloquist, Randy uses monkey puppets to tell Bible stories. After the program, the director of the orphanage brought a boy, about nine years old, to Randy. The boy reached out and hugged Randy's monkey puppet, Squeaker, as if he were a long-lost relative, jabbering with wild monkey noises and gestures.

Then the story came out. The boy, who has Down Syndrome, was born in a fishing village in the jungles of northern Cambodia. The Khmer Rouge was still active in that area in the late 1990s. They descended on the Great Lake fishing village and slaughtered most of the inhabitants, though some were able to escape to the mountains. When these returned, they assumed that the baby boy had been killed along with his dead family.

But a group of monkeys, who often came into the village at night to steal drying fish, found the baby still alive. They took him back into the jungle and nursed him. He lived with them until he was about three.

Then hunters came into the jungle, looking for monkeys. They found the human child, and brought him to the monks at a local Buddhist temple.

They tried to humanize the boy. But after a year and a half, the Buddhists decided he was too "monkeyized" for them to control. Perhaps he was being punished for the sins of a past life. They turned him out into the streets of a nearby village, where he lived like a stray dog.

Then an orphanage was being built nearby. The construction manager came to know the little monkey boy. He had compassion on him, and brought him to live in the orphanage when it was completed. He's been there for years now, loved and cared for with dignity. He's not just "monkey boy" anymore. Now he has a name: Matthias. He is in school, worships God passionately through music, and is an earnest disciple of Jesus Christ.

"We Are Hungry"

Ananthi Jebasingh, one of our friends in India, has developed a children's ministry that continues to grow beyond anyone's wildest dreams. It began, as these things often do, in a very small way.

A few years ago, Ananthi—who has a Ph.D. in linguistics— was in her middle-class home in New Delhi when there was a knock on the door. She opened it to find a small boy. "I am hungry," he said.

She gave him some food.

The next day he was back. And the day after that. Soon he was bringing friends. Twenty-five of them. They all lived in a slum area not too far from Ananthi's house. She had never been there, but she had passed by. "The stench was terrible," she says. "I would close my nose and walk away."

Ananthi fed the children. But then she felt angry with herself for not equipping them to help themselves. "I am just making beggars out of them," she thought. She prayed, and the words "We are hungry" kept echoing in her mind. She knew their deepest hunger was spiritual.

So Ananthi set up a little school in her garage. She taught the children how to read and write, and she showed them the love of Christ.

More and more children came. Ananthi had no room for them all. She went to the slum commissioner. "I can give you some space," he told her. "It's the only place we have."

He took her to the slum's public latrines. Ananthi could not believe what she was seeing and smelling. There were two unused shabby little buildings adjacent to the toilets. Piles of human waste covered the ground outside. The stench was hideous.

Ananthi and a few other Christian teachers got to work. They cleaned up the latrines. (To their great relief, God sent a strategically-timed rainstorm that washed most of the filth outside away.) They got little chairs and desks and help from some local merchants.

Slowly, gradually, they built up a little school for that slum. Yes, it sits right between the toilets—but now it is a clean, safe, secure environment for children to learn. There are now 450 students in this Christian school, right in the middle of a land that is predominantly—often militantly—Hindu.

The transformation of the latrines is a picture of the transformation of the children themselves.

As she's seen that, Ananthi's vision has grown further. Today, through our partnership and a lot of miracles, a beautiful new school is open to 2,200 children on that ground Ananthi claimed for Christ.

One Egg at a Time

It was also in India that another ministry to forgotten children began some years ago.

One morning I was sitting in a scrubby hotel in that unpronounceable town of Vijayawada. I have a strong stomach, but my less-than-five-star accommodations were casting doubt on the quality of the breakfast menu. So I ordered an egg, figuring you can't really do much to mess up an egg.

I was wrong. You can even mess up an egg if you work at it long enough.

As I tried to work my way through that egg, a young Indian man came in and sat at the table next to me. He spoke perfect English, and we entered into a conversation which I enjoyed very much. His name was B. V. Rao. I ended up asking him to join me for the day.

He interpreted for me and guided me around his city. He told me he had learned English by listening to the radio. He was exceptional in his character and conduct. Finally I asked him, "Rao, what do you do for a living?"

He reached in his wallet and pulled out his business card: *B. V. Rao, Executive Director of Prison Fellowship India.*

I've served on the board of Prison Fellowship for years—and here was this brother in the ministry traveling around with me, and we didn't even know it. I asked him if we could go into some of the local prisons.

Let the Children Come

The youth prison held children from five years old up to about seventeen. Many of these youngsters were professional thieves. They'd been taught how to pick pockets from the time they were small and then sent out to bring in income for the family. They just thought it was a way of life.

Others were in the institution only because their parents were in prison. Rather than leave them on the street, the police brought them into the dubious shelter of the children's prison.

The first room we visited was about forty-by-forty feet, without one piece of furniture. The children all slept on the floor on a dirty mat and had metal bowls from which they ate rice once a day. Flies were everywhere. There was only one toilet, and they had to walk on top of each other to get to it. They all wore shorts, no shirts, and the heat was intolerable. You couldn't move without perspiration running off of you.

As we probed a bit, we discovered that the older boys would wait in the toilet area at night. If any of the smaller children came in, they would rape them.

It was horrible. I resolved to do what I could to change it.

The warden had given Rao permission to come in regularly. Rao had looked into other options for the children. Existing orphanages did not want to accept kids who were merely neglected because of a parent's imprisonment. Nor did they want to become involved in the complex problems related to prisoners and their families.

Then, even as Rao explored these avenues, the city fathers elected him as juvenile magistrate for the city. God made that happen. Here was Rao, with such a burden for prisoners' children, and now he had the official capacity to do something about their needs.

Ellen

Corporate management consultant Pat MacMillan traveled with Dois when he returned to the juvenile prison soon after meeting Rao. As they careened toward the facility in a well-dented taxi, Dois spied a sidewalk vendor with a pushcart full of bananas.

"Please stop!" Dois called to the driver. The cab shrieked to a halt, raising a cloud of dust. Dois hopped out and made the vendor's day by buying the entire cart of bananas. He and Pat managed to wrestle them all into the trunk of the cab.

Once at the prison, they met with the warden. Pat watched as Dois quietly asked him about the children and about how the warden himself managed to work in the face of such tough challenges.

"He built a relationship," Pat says. "He didn't put the warden on the defensive. But you could see the wheels turning in his head. Dois doesn't just deal with symptoms; he goes to systems. We handed out those bananas, and Dois made sure the prison had some big fans to help with the awful heat ... but his main concern was how to protect the little children from being attacked in the night.

"So many of us are so focused on our particular mission that we miss the opportunities God is placing right in front of us," says Pat. "Dois never drops his core mission of building churches, but he walks through life asking God to show him how to make a difference for Him in each day's unexpected encounters. In that situation it meant building a Christian home for children in danger.

"T. S. Eliot said that some people have the experience and miss the meaning. Dois is always looking for God's meaning in each day's experiences—and then he's obedient to what God would have him do."

After renting a small facility, Rao and his wife began caring for some of these children. But then, just before I met him, the owner of the building terminated the lease. All the doors Rao had tried since had remained shut, and he felt bleak about the children's future.

Then we had that "chance" encounter over that incredible, inedible egg. I wasn't in the business of building children's homes, but it was clear that these youngsters needed help, and God had put Rao and me on the path together as a means to do so.

So we committed to build a church and home that would house forty boys and forty girls, with room for house parents, cooking, washing, and sleeping. It was going to be wonderful. There was only one small problem. We didn't have a way to pay for it.

But God led us to a man from New Mexico named Ken Johns. When we told Ken about these children, he was filled with compassion. Ken's heart moved for these children, and he gave the funds to build them a home.

Today, in the unpronounceable city of Vijayawada, India, when juveniles are picked up off the streets, the police don't take them to prison to be abused. Instead they turn them over to B. V. Rao's "Precious Children's Home," run by Prison Fellowship India. There they are given food, clothing, and shelter. They go to school. They reach out to the community around them—and now a church meets in the home.

The vision has grown. Prison Fellowship India now runs five Precious Children Homes. One twelve-year-old girl named Bindhu described what the ministry has meant for her and her little sister Mini: "[Before], the only option before us was to go to the streets . . . . But we thank God that we have a place at the Precious Children's Home! We are happy here, and we experience God's love through the dear ones who care for us."

I think some of our greatest times in heaven will be looking back and seeing the tapestry of how God wove the strands of our lives together. Occasionally we get to see glimpses down here. Like the incredible way God brought Rao and me together and then moved in the heart of Ken Johns at just the right time that we might build a sanctuary for prisoners' children in India–for kids who were the least of the least in the eyes of many, but beloved by Jesus. "Let the little children come to me, and do not hinder them, for the kingdom of heaven belongs to such as these" (Matt. 19:14).

Let the Children Come

Helping children is not all precious moments, sweetness, and light. Whether we're in the U.S. or abroad, usually the kids who need our help most are the ones we are drawn to least. That's what happened with our friend Mary–before the miracle.

Actually, Mary didn't even like children. She maintained a polite distance from her nieces and nephews, and avoided other children whenever possible. Children spilled drinks, broke dishes, and had things hanging out of their noses. They loudly repeated themselves a lot. Mary's opinion was that just about the time kids got interesting, they left for college.

Mary still isn't sure how she ended up teaching Sunday School. Some punishment for past sins, maybe, or God had a twisted sense of humor. At least these weren't little kids. Her class was made up of fourth graders, and most of them had mastered a few basic social graces.

Except the boys.

The fourth grade boys needed medication or something. They burped and made other rude noises. Competitively. They stood on their chairs, interrupted everyone, and had the attention span of gnats.

The head offender was named Richard. He became Mary's nemesis. When she taught about Jesus healing the demon-possessed man, Richard fell to the floor and actually made foam come out of his mouth. While the girls in the class recited their memory verses, Richard would put on a pair of Walkman headphones–without a Walkman–and play air guitar. When the lesson was from the Old Testament, he cheered every time someone was decapitated, dismembered, or had a tent peg driven through his skull.

Richard was not civilized.

Mary realized this was an opportunity for her own spiritual growth. So she prayed for Richard. She prayed he would move away.

Then she tried to reason with herself. He came from a broken home. He needed love. God had put her in Richard's life for a purpose.

She still didn't like the kid, but now her dander was up. It was like a competition–and Satan was the enemy,   not Richard. She wasn't going to let him win. She decided she had to act as though she loved Richard. She had to *do* something loving–and maybe the feelings would follow.

She didn't know what she would do. Have Richard over for dinner? The very thought of it struck terror deep into her soul. Then came a simple idea that was even worse.

The next Sunday was a lesson on Jesus' love for His disciples. Mary arrived at class with a washbasin, Yardley's English lavender soap, and a towel. She filled the basin with warm water. The class, quiet for once, gathered around her. "Jesus washed His friends' feet," she told them. "Like this." She actually knelt in front of Richard's chair. He stared at her. Unable to speak, she motioned toward his gigantic, odiferous tennis shoes. Shocked, also speechless, he removed them.

Mary took hold of Richard's huge feet and guided them into the shallow tub. As soon as she did so, she found she could talk again. In fact, she found that as she held Richard's feet, her feelings about him changed. She gently soaped his toes and buffed his heels as she told the class about Jesus' love for His disciples.

"The Kingdom of heaven belongs to such as these."

Really.

Mountains and
Mustard Seed Miracles
Dois

In 2000 we partnered with Christian leaders in Nepal to break ground on our first church building. We had encountered many difficulties in our attempts to enter Nepal, but we trusted in the Lord to open doors. Sure enough, God had a strategy in place for us to help them.

Already, in northern India near the Nepalese border, we'd met Reverend Mamman Joseph. Leader of the Peniel Gospel Team of Scripture Ministries of India, Pastor Joseph had established new congregations in the northern areas of West Bengal. One of his congregations had built a church for Nepali believers right at the India-Nepal border, and those men and women were being discipled and equipped to plant churches in their own nation.

In addition to that, God opened up another significant field of ministry in the same area: the giant tea plantations of northern India.

What God Is Brewing

These tea gardens stretch for hundreds of miles along the foothills of the Himalayan Mountains in the Indian state of West Bengal. They are adjacent to the nations of Nepal, Bhutan, Tibet, and Bangladesh. Owned by large international corporations, these plantations are staffed by thousands of workers from those countries. These men and women live right on the grounds, but eventually they return to their homelands—and we are equipping them to do so as followers of Christ.

A low mist hovers over the plantations in the early mornings. As it rises, row upon row upon row of manicured tea bushes stretch for as far as you can see. The care of the tender green leaves—which will become the world's finest teas—is absolutely meticulous.

As workers have come to know Christ through the Mini Bible College broadcasts, their bosses have noticed the changes in their lives. These managers—Hindus themselves—have said that Christians typically make better employees than non-Christians. They do not get drunk; they are respectful and cheerful in their attitudes; they have a strong work ethic. (Since, as the New Testament teaches, they work for their earthly masters "as unto the Lord.")

So, even though Christianity runs counter to the Hindu culture around them, some of the more practical tea garden managers have actively encouraged the growth of the Gospel among their workers and have given space on the plantation grounds for churches to be built.

Candles in the Night

We have visited many of these churches. One is in a remote, northern plantation; we traveled for hours on the narrow Indian roads. Darkness fell; we arrived at the church in the quietness of the night, millions of bright stars shining down from above.

Alerted to our arrival by some sort of invisible grapevine, the church members suddenly materialized. They brought an oil lamp and candles to light the night. They proudly showed us the progress on their building. Then we stood in a circle, held hands, prayed, and sang "Alleluia." I will never forget the flickering light on their faces, the strength of their grip as we stood linked together, sisters and brothers in Jesus.

"Why Is It You Care for These People?"

At another tea garden, we partnered to build the Salbari Church. The plantation manager and his wife, both Hindus, attended the dedication service. They sat in places of honor near the front and wept openly, touched in a way they had not expected, as the workers sang praises to God, laughed, danced, and listened to Pastor Joseph preach the Gospel.

Afterward the manager came to Pastor Joseph.

"Why is it you care for these people?" he asked. "How is it they have such joy?"

Pastor Joseph told him, "We love, because He first loved us."

The manager looked at the ground, his face still wet with the tears he could not explain. "Then I must know more about your Jesus," he said.

The manager soon resigned his position. He moved to the city of Shiliguri to live near Pastor Joseph. He and his wife are part of a Bible study and discipleship group, and Pastor Joseph is helping them design their own outreach plan, so they can love "these people" as Christ has loved them.

Ellen

Because of such opposition, Dois and his partners try to be careful in their visits to these areas. We visited one such village a while ago. The local pastor thought it best that just Dois and three others visit the church building under construction, rather than our whole group drawing attention to our presence in the area.

We parked our van in a side lane. No one was around.

Dois got out.

"Just stay in the van," he told us. "Don't do anything to make people notice you. Keep a low profile, and we'll be back in a few minutes."

"Of course," we said obediently. "Low profile."

He strode off to inspect the church building. As they did, the van driver decided to turn the vehicle around, so it would be ready for a quick exit if need be. But in so doing, he backed up too far. His rear wheels got stuck in a deep patch of sand. He panicked, gunned the motor, and spun the wheels even deeper. The van was hopelessly stuck.

By the time Dois and the others returned from their clandestine visit to the church, they saw a huge mob of people surrounding the van. Dois broke into a run. Men with turbans and no teeth were shouting wildly in Bengali. Women in saris, carrying babies, were pointing in opposite directions. Children were jumping up and down and shrieking with excitement.

Young men in loincloths were digging under the van's rear wheels; others had brought long pieces of wood that they were shoving underneath it. Motor scooters were everywhere, with more people arriving at the scene with each passing moment.

The entire village, it seemed, had come to rescue our stuck van.

Meanwhile, one of our group started pulling kids' jump ropes from her enormous purse and handing them out to the village children. Their mothers were crowding around us, curiously holding our hands up to look at our wedding rings and laughing at our clothes.

We smiled sheepishly when we saw Dois coming.

"Oh, Dois," we said, "we're so sorry the low profile thing didn't work out!"

Then the men all joined in together, Hindus and Christians side by side, and put their shoulders to the back of the van. They all shouted, "Heave, ho!" in various languages. Our driver gunned the motor, and with a great shower of sand on everyone, the vehicle shook and then shot out of the hole.

Everyone cheered; we shook hands all around, piled into the van, and made our getaway.

It's probably not a great evangelistic technique, but our "low profile" visit evoked sufficient curiosity to raise church attendance the following Sunday. Meanwhile we saw, yet again, that God can use anything for His purposes.

Walking the Walk

In some of these areas there were no believers at all. Burdened for one village in particular, Pastor Joseph and some fellow Christians began visiting it regularly. They would walk through the village, praying silently as they strolled, smiling and nodding to people as they passed. After some time of preparing the ground, so to speak, they began preaching outdoors.

The villagers were intrigued by the stories of Jesus, but they were cautious. By the end of six months of prayer and preaching by the Gospel team, three families had proclaimed their commitment to follow Christ. They started a regular evening meeting, which grew into a small congregation–and now there are more than eighty believers in that village.

What's more, they have planted outposts. Many villages in the Himalayan foothills cannot be accessed by vehicles. You have to walk to them. So these believers have hiked up into the mountain villages, planting four little outstation churches. Another eighty believers are part of these Nepali-speaking congregations.

Another northern India village, Naxalbari, has long been a training center for militant political activists. Smuggling arms and planting explosives, they had terrorized various parts of India. But now there is a new church there. Twenty-six new believers were just baptized, and the church body continues to grow.

But not without opposition.

Though India's constitution provides for religious tolerance, in some places local government casts a blind eye to militant Hindu persecution of Christians, as we mentioned already in the story about Gujarat. Believers sometimes hold baptisms of new converts under cover of darkness, since Christians have been harassed and beaten.

Some churches have been sabotaged. In other areas enemies of the church have blocked roads so construction vehicles could not get through.

Mustard Seed Faith

The little churches we've built in the foothills of Nepal and the tea plantations of northern India have shown me the truth of Jesus' words. "I tell you the truth," Jesus said to His disciples, "if you have faith as small as a mustard seed, you can say to this mountain, 'Move from here to there' and it will move. Nothing will be impossible for you" (Matt. 17:20).

Consider the immensity of Everest, or even of the low-rise middle eastern peak that Jesus likely gestured toward when He said these words. My brain cannot conceive of the disparity between a mountain five miles high and a mustard seed, which is about the size of the period at the end of this sentence.

What did Jesus mean?

He said this after the disciples had been unable to heal a little boy. "Why couldn't we do it?" they asked Him. "Because you have so little faith," Jesus told them plainly.

Hebrews 11 tells us that "faith is being sure of what we hope for and certain of what we do not see." The chapter goes on to list the great heroes of faith of the Old Testament, a motley crew of ordinary men and women who somehow had a particle of faith to believe in God's invisible power–against the visible evidence to the contrary that was right in front of them.

Take our favorite hero Abraham. He obeyed God even though he did not know where he was going. He believed God even though he was elderly and "as good as dead."

And what happened? God used him to found a great nation.

That same dynamic has clearly been the case in our ministry. Often we have not known where we were going. Often, in strange time zones and bleak conditions, we have felt "as good as dead." Yet God has taken our mustard seed of faith and done miracles.

Not that He has moved any mountain ranges. Yet.

No, when Jesus told His disciples that a tiny point of faith could move a mountain, I don't think He was speaking literally. Of course He could move any mountain if He wanted to. But He often used vivid metaphors to make startling points. He was saying that even a little bit of faith–believing an invisible God at His word, contrary to the physical evidence around us–can make miracles happen. (Evidently, in the Matthew 17 account, the disciples didn't even have *that* amount of faith.)

What was key, of course, was not the amount of the faith but the *object* of the faith: the powerful, living God. Believe in Him, and stand back!

"Little People Change the World"

When we were in Calcutta a few years ago, we visited Mother Teresa's convent. We met with Sister Margaret Mary, an energetic nun from Bangladesh who had been one of the first

Missionaries of Charity when Mother Teresa founded her order in the early 1950s.

Wearing her order's white sari with blue borders, Sister Margaret Mary told us about their beginnings, when she and other young novices struggled with their choice to live as the poorest of the poor.

She talked about how visitors now come from all over the world to the convent, about the 124 countries in which the order is established, with its thousands of nuns. She spoke of the 74,000 people Nirmal Hriday, the House of the Dying, has taken off the streets of Calcutta, and how each one has been loved in the name of Christ and tenderly enabled to die in a place of security.

"Seventy-four thousand!" she said. "But it all started with *one*."

Then she leaned forward and motioned toward a large color photograph of Mother Teresa that was hanging on the wall. The tiny, wrinkled nun looked about four feet tall. "I'll tell you this," Sister Margaret Mary said to us, pointing at Mother Teresa, "Little people change the world!"

As the apostle Paul wrote, the message of the Cross itself seems "foolishness to some, a stumbling block to the pride of others; but to those whom God has called, it is the power and the wisdom of God. For the foolishness of God is wiser than man's wisdom, and the weakness of God is stronger than man's strength. God chose the foolish things of the world to shame the wise; God chose the weak things of the world to shame the strong" (1 Cor. 1:25-27).

Jesus didn't gallop onto the world scene and depose the Romans with a blinding display of His powers. He came as an ordinary person. He allowed Himself to die the most ignoble death. And when He talked about His Kingdom, He didn't say that it was like a victorious advancing army mowing down its enemies.

No, He said it is like a tiny mustard seed, of all things. The smallest of seeds–which slowly grows to become the greatest   of trees.

Here come those great, counterintuitive paradoxes of Christianity again. We cannot grasp the Gospel unless we are willing to embrace them!

The more I see how Christ builds His Church around the world today, the more I realize that it is through ordinary, often slow-growing, organic means. Not through great campaigns designed by the best marketing planners North America has to offer, but through lives changed one by one by one.

That's how things go in the midst of God's great unfolding history of grace. Right now.

But it's not the end of the story. In the end, Christ will come again in great glory. The Lamb will be the Lion of Judah, and every eye will see Him. Every knee will bow. Every person will confess that He is Lord. And the King of the great conquering Kingdom will reign forever.

But for now, He does His miracles in quieter ways. He builds His Church through mustard seed miracles–and yes, as Sister Mary Margaret says–He uses little people to change the world.

Part 3: The Commission: "As You Are Going"

Tools for the Road
Ellen

What mountain lies in your path, blocking your way to new heights with Christ? Can you go around it? Can you scale it, step by step? Will God move it by the speck of your mustard-seed faith?

What I've seen in Dois's work around the world–and the wild characters God has connected Dois with–is that no miracle is too big, or too small, for God. The only impediments we have, like bowling balls bound to our hiking boots, are our fears and the failure to believe that God is really God. He'll move mountains if need be. Or He'll cut steps so we can climb them. The view from the top is magnificent.

That's great news. It means we don't have to be extraordinary to do extraordinary things. *God* is extraordinary. We just need to be *available.*

Then He'll use us wherever we are. We needn't go to Nepal . . . unless, of course, He calls us there. He'll use us in suburbia, in the city, in our businesses, schools, and neighborhoods. He'll give us the grace to wash fourth-grade feet, to open our homes to the up-and-out, to entertain strangers, or to lead a prison Bible study or a teenaged youth group. He'll use us wherever we are and wherever we go.

After all, that's the essence of the marching orders for every Christian—the Great Commission.

Just before His ascension, Jesus said, "Go into all the world and preach the good news to all creation . . . . Go and make disciples of all nations, baptizing them in the name of the Father and of the Son and of the Holy Spirit" (Mark 16:15; Matt. 28:19).

Some people have read that well-known passage as if it's for a select few who are to go to foreign lands. And Jesus' command *is* a special call for those God leads into full-time missions as a vocation.

But it's also a general commission for all of us. In the Greek, the verb tense of "go" is better translated "having gone," "when you go," or *"as you are going."* The primary verb is "make disciples." Jesus assumed His people would be going here, there, and everywhere; the command He took pains to give was that we spread His good news and make disciples as we go.

"As you are going"—to work, to school, on errands, wherever. *As you are going,* preach the Gospel, using words if necessary, as St. Francis said. We are to lift Jesus up, drawing others to Him by our likeness of His love.

So, as we conclude this book, and *as you are going,* here are a few closing thoughts from Dois. Think of them as tools to take on the road.

Look Under Rocks
Dois

Only God knows what I would be doing today if I had not met Dick Woodward. Perhaps I'd be teeing off at Pebble Beach or cruising the international waterway or, more likely, looking for another piece of land to develop as I called my office three times a day to see how sales were going this month.

But God had other plans. Back on that fateful day in 1979, I innocently attended a prayer breakfast led by a harmless-looking pastor. And through Dick Woodward's Bible teaching, God turned my life upside down.

None of what has happened since, in terms of building churches, funding schools and orphanages, and building up the Body around the world has happened because I'm so sharp. God equipped me for what He wanted me to do, yes, but God's power flows in unusual ways only as we realize that apart from Him, we can do nothing.

No one has been more surprised than Dick and I to see what God has done through us and in spite of us. As a car dealer and a land developer, I never dreamed I could be fulfilling the Great Commission in foreign lands. As a local pastor and then a quadriplegic, Dick never dreamed his Bible teaching would spread around the world.

So we have seen how God works miracles through ordinary people.

To put it in a really crass way, we both feel that if God can use a cripple and a used-car salesman to build His Church all over the world, He can use *anyone*.

One of the greatest habits we can develop on our journey through this life is one of the simplest. We've referred to it in this book, but now let me formally announce it as a principle to live by:

Look Under Rocks!

I've used this standard for years in my businesses. I keep my eyes open for any opportunity that might be out there–though not necessarily in plain sight. As I look under the rocks of my everyday experiences, I find all kinds of possibilities for development. I evaluate them in light of ultimate goals. If they match, I take action to pursue them.

A Clamp Unto My Feet

For example, years ago I found out about a tool used during World War II for shipbuilding. It was a clamp, made by the thousands and sent to shipyards all over the country. But then it became obsolete, useless for the ships built after the war. The company that made it went out of business.

I ran down the patent and, after some negotiations, bought it for $2,800. I'm sure the owner considered me a friend for life.

But then a friend and I worked together, testing and fiddling with the design over hundreds of hours. In the end, we successfully upgraded it so it could be used for modern shipbuilding.

And for the last twenty years, I don't believe any major ship, submarine, or aircraft carrier built in this country–or in many other parts of the world–has been constructed without the use of that little tool we re-designed. It's called a Jack Clamp. It has funded my children's college and postgraduate education and far, far more.

I applied the principle of looking under business rocks for years before it occurred to me that I should do it in all things.

None of My Business

I've mentioned several times how I used to divide my life into two categories: Kingdom business and my everyday business of selling cars and developing real estate.

Well, it's a very simple point, but it took me years to really get it: There is no such compartmentalization. It's not as though Sundays belong to God and my work week belongs to me. None of it is mine. It's all God's business. He cares about it all. He owns it all. And He can use it all.

We all know this intellectually. But when we really grab hold of it and live the fact that everything we have, everything we do, belongs to God, it will revolutionize our lives. It will free us to try to see what He is doing–and how we can become a part of it.

That means we have no chance encounters. No ordinary days. Even as we change the oil in the car, wash dishes, fill out the tax forms, mow the lawn, make the business decision, write the brief, take a walk with the neighbor, whatever it is, God is with us! God loves us! He doesn't waste anything, but is at work all over the world, even at the very moment you are reading this paragraph, for His purposes!

What Would You Have Me Do?

Helen Keller was blind from infancy. She could not hear. She could not speak. Yet later in her life, after she had been equipped by caring people to recognize the opportunities God had for her, she wrote this:

> For His sake: I am but one, but I am one.
> I cannot do everything, but I can do something.
> What I can do, I ought to do.
> What I ought to do, by the grace of God I will do.
> *Lord, what will you have me do?*

Delivered Right to Our Door

Sometimes we don't even need to turn over a rock to find a new possibility. Often God brings them right to us.

For example, I told you how in 1992 my friend Bob Daley brought his Vietnamese buddy Vang Le into my office. I wasn't expecting it—but it was the God-given key that opened the door to building churches all over Vietnam.

Similarly, God unexpectedly led us to build those church-orphanages in Cambodia. The same thing happened with the homes for prisoners' children in India. All the stories we've told in this book never would have happened if it had been left up to *us* and *our* plans. We picked up the rocks God put in front of us.

What Should I Do?

Our friend, the late Dr. Richard Halverson, chaplain of the United States Senate, pastor, writer, teacher, mentor, was once asked how in the world he accomplished all the things he did. It was almost as if the questioner had her Day-Timer in one hand, a cell phone in the other, trying to figure out how Dick had such peace in the midst of a very busy life. Was it scheduling? Delegating? Or was it a matter of getting just the right Palm Pilot?

Dick paused for moment as if he were surprised by the question. "I only do one thing," he said. "And that is to follow Christ."

In reality, many of us balk at that. We want a formula, a day-to-day schedule to follow. But following Christ is not a matter of a to-do list, checking off the boxes. It is a matter of a relationship with Jesus and obedience to the nudge of His Holy Spirit in all things.

Obey the Prompt

Let me use an imperfect illustration. God designed us with certain capabilities. As human beings, our hardware, if you will, is essentially the same, from person to person, all over the world. Then if we have committed our lives to Christ and chosen to follow Him, His software is in us. And His Holy Spirit will prompt us with certain defaults, but we must still choose to obey those prompts.

The beautiful thing about God's "software" is that it produces unique results in each person. The Holy Spirit prompts us all to uniform standards of holiness. We are told that believers will exhibit the same character traits as our Designer: love, joy, peace, goodness, self-control, patience, and so on.

But those shared traits will be manifest in unique ways in each of us, according to our personalities.

Which Rocks Do I Pick Up?

What I have found is that as we become who God has called us to be, God is faithful to lead us to the specific things He'd have us do. There's no formula. He reveals His will in quiet ways, in the intimacy of our relationship with Him.

Often we want instant answers so we can charge off to do the next thing. Sometimes we read the Bible as if it's a vending machine–you know, punch a button, claim a verse, and a promise pops out. Only as we are willing to wait on the Lord does the Holy Spirit burn a particular leading from Scripture into our hearts.

So, as we purposefully seek Him out, earnestly submitting our will to His, He will lead us. He doesn't write messages in the sky. But He opens some doors. He closes others. He confirms our path through the wisdom of Christian friends. And He confirms His will through the gift of peace–certainty about what choices He's nudging us to make, what opportunities we should pick up, what mountains we should climb. His peace empowers us even as we feel we cannot go forward in our own inadequate strength.

So feel free: Turn over rocks. God will give you the strength to pick them up.

War Footing
Dois

Another essential tool for life on the road is a sense of holy urgency. We must maintain our *"war footing."* This is a term we've heard much more frequently in the U.S. since our nation has been at war with terrorism. It is the way military men and women describe personal combat readiness–a state of high alert in which one is prepared to engage the enemy, ready for action.

Spiritual soldiers should maintain their war footing as well. Our time on earth is not a leisurely stroll. God has placed us here for a purpose; we need to march at an urgent pace. We don't know how much time we have left.

I thought of this when I had to go into the hospital a while ago.

I hate hospitals. But I had been getting up at four o'clock in the morning every day, traveling a lot, and eating strange food in foreign countries. Somewhere along the line, my lungs contracted an aggressive infection. They let me know of their irritation by shutting down. Shirley called 911.

I awoke, much to my dismay, in the emergency room, with tubes and wires and machines monitoring my every breath.

I survived. So far.

Ellen

Some years ago Craig, a young man Dois had mentored, accompanied him to a men's retreat where Dois was speaking. Most of the guys there were affluent, retired businessmen. After Dois's first talk, one attendee turned to Craig.

"Man, that's great," he said. "I'd love to do some kind of ministry like Dois."

"Why can't you?" asked Craig, never one to miss an opportunity to be blunt.

"Well," said the man, "I'm getting older, you know."

"If you don't mind my asking, how old are you?" Craig asked.

"I'm seventy-one," he said.

"Oh," said Craig. "Dois is eighty."

The man's eyebrows went up. He coughed. "The other thing is, it's a little late in life to get started with something new."

"Dois was sixty-five when he started full-time ministry," said Craig cheerfully.

"And then there's my health," the man continued, ever so slightly irked. "My doctor says I need to avoid stress on my heart."

Craig tried to restrain himself but failed. "Well, Dois had two heart attacks back to back when he was in his forties."

"Excuse me," the man said. "Wonderful to chat with you, but I just remembered I need to be somewhere else."

As Samuel Johnson said, the hangman's noose marvelously concentrates the mind. So does a hospital visit. When you're horizontal, staring at a video monitor's jiggling image of your own heartbeat, you realize how easily it could stop. You gain a fresh sense of urgency for what is really important in this life.

If my friends in their forties are in halftime, as Bob Buford calls midlife, then I've already heard the two-minute warning.

So a sense of life's brevity propels me forward.

I get the same sense of urgency when I consider what's going on around the world. When we started building churches in the late 1980s, we didn't know what would develop in some of the countries where we were working. Now reports come in every day about churches that have been attacked, believers who have been persecuted, bombs being placed where Christians gather.

A pastor named Yesu Dasu lived in an area where extremists of another religion are hostile to Christianity. Two men came to his home one evening, saying that a friend needed help. He went with them.

Hours went by; his wife and four children became more and more concerned. Finally the next morning, his mutilated body was found outside the village. He had been hacked with an axe and beheaded. He was fifty-two years old.

Yesu Dasu did not know that autumn evening would be his last on this earth. But when his time came, he was at his post, doing the work to which he had been called.

I can only hope the same will be said for me, however the end comes.

We have partners in a country that is politically volatile. These men and women invest themselves in ministry day and night. Their pace is extraordinary.

Why? One pastor told me, "We don't know how long the opportunity will be open for us. If the government changes, we will no longer have the freedom to build churches and preach the Gospel openly. We must do everything we can, while we still can."

There's another very practical aspect of urgency: costs are going up.

Many of the countries in which we work are ripe for development. Right now we can build a lot for a little. So the sooner we break ground, the more we can build for our investment.

For example, churches in Vietnam that seat a hundred people cost $5,000. One church we built in the highlands there seats more than 1,500 people. It cost $70,000. In the U.S. that same facility would have a price tag of more than a million dollars. And that Vietnamese church and its daughter congregations now have more than 17,000 members.

In India, a church for 200 people costs $7,000.

A Cambodian orphanage that shelters about fifty children, with an attached church capacity for 200 people, costs about $30,000.

In China, we're building places of worship that accommodate 500 people–for a budget around $30,000.

As a businessman, I see those as good opportunities. I've tried to move in and take advantage of them before these countries become more developed and building costs rise.

Another thing that compels me is the fact that Jesus is coming back. You don't hear much about that today. Men and women of earlier generations had a sense of Christ's imminent return that compelled them to spend their lives in the hellholes of the world. We should have no less a sense of urgency.

I feel that if we fail to build a church where God is calling us, people may be lost for eternity. If we fail to bring the Gospel to

---

Ellen

To spur his own sense of Kingdom urgency, Pat MacMillan keeps a photograph of Dois on his desk. It was taken in that dysfunctional Russian helicopter that transported us in Cambodia. We had been "flying" all over the countryside in it for two days. The heat and the pace had been draining. Most of us were dozing or had passed out from the terror of imminent death.

Pat snapped a photo of Dois in a different mode: as the engines roared and the winds rushed by the open porthole, Dois looked out over the land of Cambodia, eyes narrowed and lips moving in a prayer only God could hear. And if he could, he would have made that old chopper fly faster.

"While we all rested," says Pat, "Dois was pressing on, thinking about the next step, about how to do it better, faster, cheaper, and what to do with that last rock he just picked up."

those lives God brings into our realm of influence, then we are remiss in what He has asked us to do.

I have to ask myself, "How many ways am I really sharing the Gospel?" He died for us so we might spend eternity with Him. Every day that we delay that message, souls are being lost.

That doesn't mean that we go at a chaotic pace, however. I think the Lord expects us to be effective and efficient even as we march to an urgent cadence. I pray for that daily.

After all, if Coca Cola can put cola in every village of the world, then we can put the Gospel there. The same technology that enables Coke executives to spread the cola is available to us to advance the Kingdom of God.

Some days I think in terms of, "Lord, why don't you just give us all we need right now so we can just go into village after village as expeditiously as we know how?"

I don't understand why not. But the one thing I do understand is that Jesus would have us do everything we *can* do each day for Him. And then we go home and rest and start again the next day.

We use every tool. It doesn't mean we have to go to some far-away place. It does mean that *as we are going* about the things of each day, pastor and layperson alike, we use everything we have.

We use *every* resource, *every* bit of energy, *all* our abilities, *every* opportunity–that we might *be* the people of Christ-like character He would have us be, and *do* all that He calls us to do.

Then, by His grace, when the end comes, we'll see His smile and hear His promised words: "Well done, good and faithful servant!"

I love this quote from C. T. Studd:

> "Let us not rust out. Let us not glide through the world and then slip quietly out, without having blown the trumpet loud and long for our blessed Redeemer. At the very least, let us see to it that the devil holds a thanksgiving in hell when he gets the news of our departure from the field of battle."

Transforming Nations

Dois

When people used to ask me about our ministry, I would say that we were in the business of reproducing congregations. That's exciting in itself, as new churches grow and in turn plant daughter flocks.

But something even bigger is going on. God is doing much more than starting new groups of believers, significant as that is. He is building His Body around the world today, toward the end that communities, states, and entire countries might actually be transformed from the inside out.

So now I think in bolder terms. Through this small work of building churches and broadcasting the Gospel, *God is transforming nations.*

Interestingly, some of the countries where we see that most clearly are those that have been the last communist holdouts on the globe.

Like Vietnam. We've told you a little bit about the explosion of the Gospel there and how churches are multiplying across that land. In one church in Ho Chi Minh City, thousands of people attended five Easter services More than 250 made public commitments to Jesus Christ that day.

And when members of the British Parliament toured Vietnam, communist officials took the dignitaries to see "their" church—as a showcase example of what is happening in the "new" Vietnam. (Soon afterward the government formally recognized, for the first time, the Evangelical Church of Vietnam.)

Through the growth, planting, and new construction of these evangelical churches, communities of believers are growing up all over Vietnam, particularly in the south. In some tribal areas, we're building chapels in the middle of soybean fields, where peasants use oxen to plow their soil, and things haven't changed much since the late 19th century. These little churches are the center of their rural communities.

In the big cities, the modern churches we build seat thousands of people. One has planted five new churches and baptizes about 200 new believers every year. Another grew from 300 to 600 members, and planted and built three new daughter churches of 100 members each, in just a few years' time.

Wherever they are, and whatever size, these churches are doing whatever they can to help the people who live nearby. Because of that, they are seen as an asset to their communities by government officials . . . and are allowed to continue to preach the Gospel.

In China, the situation is similarly complex, but on a much bigger scale. During a recent trip there, I felt an incredible sense of energy in the air . . . everywhere I went in the cities, I saw construction, development, and business investment as Beijing prepared to host the 2008 Olympic Games. Seventy-five percent of the world's construction cranes are soaring into China's skyline. Someone told me that 55 percent of the world's concrete is in China. Thousands of workers were building highways, hotels, arenas, and restaurants.

Something new is happening *spiritually* in China as well. The Spirit of God is moving in fresh ways. Far more than Olympic venues are being built; Chinese believers are constructing hundreds of brand-new local churches in which to worship God and preach His Word.

While many of us are familiar with the great stories of faith and courage of the past, now there are *new* stories to be told . . . about the *registered* church, and the unprecedented freedoms its believers now have . . . freedom to build their own churches, to preach the Gospel, and welcome new believers into their congregations.

In many areas, government officials have seen how believers help meet the physical and social needs in their communities. They are allowing—on a case-by-case basis—our Chinese partners to build and plant new churches at an unprecedented rate.

The Gospel seeds that brave missionaries and Chinese pastors planted many years ago are now bearing new fruit that will transform lives for generations to come. Sometimes Americans think of the Church in China as populated by gray-hair ladies . . . but during a recent trip, I was struck by how many of our brand-new churches there were overflowing with believers of all ages, including many young people who have come to faith in Christ over the last few years.

We met with an energetic pastor whose church has grown from a handful of believers to a body of 600 people from nearby villages. They've bought a piece of land right next to the main highway in their town. When their church is built, it will shine like a beacon to tens of thousands of people in that rural area.

As I write, I have the happy problem of knowing that any statistics I quote will soon be out of date, because the work of church-building is progressing so rapidly. But I'll go for it anyway. Right now, 300 churches have been built or are under construction by ICM's Chinese partners. The Chinese Christian leaders we're working with plan to bring that total to 500 churches soon, and they are planning to build hundreds more in the coming years.

Our Chinese brothers and sisters are planting new churches in rural areas that haven't yet experienced the economic boom taking place in China's major cities. The approach is to build big churches in the larger rural cities first . . . the equivalent of what we know as "county seats." These larger congregations are then surrounded by smaller daughter churches. Entire regions can be transformed as these clusters of churches reach out to meet the physical, educational, and spiritual needs of the disadvantaged people who live nearby. Then, as people come to know Christ, the churches also serve as centers for in-depth pastoral and lay leader training, fellowship, and accountability. Then they reproduce themselves by planting more daughter churches.

China's economic development and place on the world stage at the Olympics make it open and ready for business in unprecedented ways. And at the moment it's open for *Kingdom business* as well. It's a door of opportunity that our Chinese partners urge us to use right now for the glory of God.

The same thing is happening in Cuba, which is a spiritual petri dish–a self-contained location that demonstrates the culture-changing power of the Church. Soon we will have built or rebuilt a church every twelve and a half miles across that island, with each one planting at least five more.

We can't typecast Cuba; it is changing daily. But it's not the place it was ten years ago. It's crackling with the power of the Holy Spirit. Whole communities have been changed–and God's power is leaping across that island like an electrical current.

Once the Soviet Union fell, Cuba lost its primary financial support. In the years that followed, the government there eased more in order to draw in tourists from South America, Europe, and Canada. Then in 1992, Fidel Castro changed the constitution to declare that Cuba was no longer officially an "atheist" state but a "secular" one. More recent government documents state that Santeria is Cuba's "official cultural religion." Santeria's origins lie in African idol worship and animal sacrifice. It was brought to the island by slaves during the eighteenth century. The government gives Santeria proponents radio and TV time; 75 percent of Christianity's new believers on the island convert from Santeria's shadowy practices.

John Paul II's 1998 visit provided a wedge for Christian expression; the government allowed the Pope to conduct a huge open-air mass in Havana's Revolution Square. Afterward–to the immense delight of Cuban children–Castro reinstated the celebration of Christmas. A year later evangelicals were allowed to hold a huge meeting in the same location. "It's as if he [Castro] opened the box," one Cuban pastor told me, "and now he cannot force it shut again."

It's a complicated situation, neither all bad news nor all good. The government sometimes hassles Christians. Informers still do their work. Building permits for new churches are routinely denied. Electrical power sometimes shuts down mysteriously when there's a Christian meeting.

But, as one pastor said about his congregation's wait to receive a building permit, "We just work within the things the government *does* allow us to do. We wait. We're kind of like the children of Israel in the Old Testament. We move when the cloud moves. So we build when the government lets us."

Meanwhile church membership is growing rapidly, with 70 percent of new members below the age of thirty. Castro's old revolutionary slogans hold little meaning for many young people. They long for more. Like Cecelia, a young woman who converted at sixteen. "I *knew* there was a God, even though I had been told He did not exist," she says today. She sought out a Christian girl at school, who took her to Havana's Marianao church, where Cecelia heard the Gospel and received Christ.

Marianao's pastor, Ricardo Pereira, is Bishop of the Methodist Church in Cuba. His 870-member church is one of the first we renovated in Cuba. It is the spiritual home of doctors, teachers, former prostitutes, ex-prisoners, children, men, and women of every background.

During one visit to Cuba, we were assigned a "tour guide," a government official who traveled with us to churches all over the island in order to monitor just what we were up to. He accompanied us to the Mariano church.

More than eight hundred people were already packed into the sanctuary. Ushers took us up to the front, where shimmering music poured from the young people leading worship. Liturgical dancers shook tambourines with long streamers of red and gold. The air moved with the breezes of hundreds of people fanning themselves.

Down the long center aisle came people bearing the communion bread and wine, led by dancers holding huge banners aloft: *Pan de vida.* Bread of Life. *Vino nuevo.* New wine. And in the midst of the procession came Ricardo in his purple shirt, white collar, black and red vestments flowing behind him, the shepherd of the flock.

He told the crowd about the visitors from North America who were helping to build churches all over Cuba. "What is life?" Ricardo continued. "What will be left of my life? We don't know when it will end. This is the moment to put our lives in front of God, and consider what fruits they are bearing for Him."

Then, as Ricardo read Psalm 23, we took communion two by two, North Americans and Cubans celebrating the body and blood of Christ together.

Afterward Ricardo asked anyone who wanted to commit his or her life to Christ to come forward. From the back row, an unshaven man wearing muddy boots began the long walk toward the front.

Ricardo rushed down the aisle and escorted the man forward. Then a little girl, about ten years old, stepped out of her pew. Then a teenager walked down the aisle. As they arrived at the front, we leaned out of our pews to hug each one. New brothers and a sister in Christ.

As the service ended, we saw our tour guide listening intently. Usually Felix waited out in the bus while we were in church. But today the Spirit was at work in his heart. He was weeping.

That evening we traveled to a drab complex of four-story apartment blocks on the outskirts of Havana. A pastor named Juan had started a house church there. A small group of believers had become ten, then twenty, thirty, forty, fifty . . . and now, as we arrived, hundreds of people welcomed us. We passed through a simple apartment to a courtyard in the back–which was absolutely jammed. A chain link fence marked the boundary to the back of the unit, and dozens more were packed behind the fence. The music was electrifying, the worship strong and passionate, yet pensive.

There was a silence. Then Pastor Juan took the microphone, and to our surprise, spoke in English. He spoke directly to our friendly communist tour guide, who was sitting on a palm-wood bench, listening intently.

"Felix," said Juan, "You have been traveling with our friends from North America all week. You have had the opportunity to hear the ministry of the Word. You have heard the truth that God loves you. And so, Felix, I have only one question for you.

"Do you choose to receive Jesus Christ? It is simple: Which will it be? Yes or no?"

There was a silence. Felix looked down at the ground, then spread his hands, palms upward.

"Yes," he said. He stood, walked forward, and the crowd cheered as a new brother came home to the Father.

Such prodigals are coming to faith all over the world . . . even in Muslim nations. We're quietly at work in a number of Muslim countries, where the Holy Spirit is at work in all kinds of ways that cannot yet be reported. As we've said, the Mini Bible College in Arabic is available to a potential audience of 285 million Arabic-speaking people. In addition to radio broadcasting, unlimited access to MBC material is available on the Internet. We get emails every day from believers in "closed" countries who are studying the Word of God online.

We often don't know what God is doing through the broadcasting and Internet downloading, but we *do* know that His Word will not return empty. It *will* accomplish His purposes.

I take heart even in those times of great severity and great opportunity as all of us yearn to proclaim God's healing love to a broken world. God calls us to be faithful. And then, through our small human efforts, He *will* build His Church.

The Choice

Ellen

We opened this book with stories from the killing fields of Cambodia. My first visit there, six years ago, was unforgettable . . . if not for that death-defying, ancient Russian helicopter, then certainly because of the unmistakable evidence of how God's love really brings life and hope to places of death and darkness.

So I was curious to return to Southeast Asia with Dois a half-dozen years later. What would be the same? What would be different?

One thing that didn't change was Dois's relentless desire to build up the Body of Christ around the world. In spite of jet lag, 100 percent humidity, advanced age, and the specter of being served a local delicacy, fried tarantulas, Dois traveled throughout Cambodia eager to see what God was up to. "What is He going to show us today?" he would say. "What do you see?"

Here's what I saw.

First, Cambodia's economy is still scarred from the 1970s, when the Khmer Rouge obliterated schools, factories, technology, and just about every other kind of societal infrastructure. Such destruction is not easily rebuilt, particularly since Cambodia lacks the natural resources that are abundant in neighboring nations, including accessible sources of electrical power.

But Cambodia's national spirit is scarred even more deeply, torn by the slaughter of millions of innocent citizens. Men and women who were children when they saw their parents slaughtered by Pol Pot's soldiers still endure nightmares and flashbacks. Other Cambodians who perpetrated or participated in such horrors live with awful guilt. Meanwhile, the killing fields and torture cells are now sightseeing attractions, bringing in tourists from Europe and North America. The heaps of skulls and dry bones stand as silent monuments to the terrible question: *Why?*

ICM's partners in Phnom Penh, Ted and Sou Olbrich, say that many Cambodians have found no solace in their understanding of their national religion, Buddhism. They've been told that people live out the consequences of deeds in a past life. Human beings are born to suffer; only when a person reaches perfection can he or she end the cycle of constant reincarnation. Salvation comes from following the eight-fold path of perfect righteousness: right behavior, right judgment, right speech, and so forth.

It's a daunting challenge . . . depending on your deeds, you'll be reincarnated as a higher or lower life form. Bad deeds might make you a cockroach or a rat the next time around. You get what you deserve.

Many can't reconcile this belief system with the terrible sufferings of their people. They want to know *why* Cambodia lost a third of its population to murder, starvation, and mayhem . . . but their neighboring countries did not. "What did *we* do to deserve such pain?" they say. "If it's punishment, what hope is there of ever becoming righteous enough to escape such suffering?"

The Olbrichs say that such questions open the door wide to the Gospel of Jesus. The Cambodian pastors they work with tell people the bad news first: No, there isn't any human hope for us to become righteous enough to earn salvation. No one is good enough to escape the cycle of suffering.

Then comes the good news: No one, that is, except the actual son of God, who came to earth and lived life perfectly. "We can piggyback on His good works," they say. "We can become perfectly righteous, not because of what we do, but because of what Jesus has already done. He's our only hope for escaping the cycle of suffering and death, the only hope for heaven."

He's also the only hope for living with freedom and joy right now. Today, throughout Cambodia, the original church-orphanages from six years ago are not only bursting at the seams, they've spawned daughter orphanages all over the countryside. Today there are more than 100 such church-orphanages in Cambodia. They've been welcomed into towns and villages even where there are not yet Christians, for they're known as "the church that cares for children."

A few years ago, a Cambodian woman found a baby boy lying on the dirty pavement of a traffic intersection. She took pity on him and brought him to the only place she knew that could help him . . . "the church that cares for children." The orphanage welcomed him in. The kids there felt badly for him, though, since no one knew his name or where he'd been born. So they gave him Jesus' birthplace, and named him Nazareth. Today Nazareth is a happy, sturdy boy who wants to be a pastor when he grows up.

Today when new orphanages are built, they include a fish pond in the back yard so fish can be harvested and sold for profit. Near the fishponds are pig pens, where pigs are doing what pigs do best, eating, reproducing, and being sold in the local markets. The children also help to care for chickens, ducks, and rabbits on these booming farmlets.

Other orphanages have developed industries like tractor rehab and furniture construction. There's now a church-sponsored rice mill in northern Cambodia, built with donated parts and helping the orphanages become self-sufficient. (All told, the church orphans in Cambodia eat two tons of rice a day; the ever-fattening pigs get the rice hulls.)

In the central church and training center in Phnom Penh, kids are learning computer skills, music, sewing and traditional Cambodian crafts. They learn English, which gives them advantages in getting good jobs. Some have gone into dental training; a number of young men are studying to become pastors.

Meanwhile, Ted Olbrich has looked at an opportunity in front of him in Phnom Penh, and like Dois, picked it up to consider what God might have him do with it. In recent years a number of hip clothing stores have established garment factories in Cambodia since labor costs are so cheap there. There are about a quarter of a million young women who work at these centers. They live in dismal, factory-provided housing and sew blue jeans for 12 hours a day, six days a week, for about $70 U.S. a month. They send most of that money home to their families, who live in poor villages in the countryside.

Moved by compassion for these "factory girls," Ted is working on a government permit to build a series of dorms for them–healthy, secure church homes in which they'll be cared for, learn about the love of Christ, and eventually be trained to share their faith in their workplaces.

Ted believes that God will do wonderful things through this outreach. "I just keep putting one foot in front of the other," he says. "But what I see is that God's work here is bearing great fruit! In the past seven years, the movement here has grown to 400,000 believers in Cambodia's 23 provinces. Some districts are now almost 30 percent Christian."

In one village where many people had come to Christ, the Buddhist monks (who eat by begging food on the street from local Buddhists) had been going hungry, because there just weren't enough Buddhists left to feed them. The local church decided to feed the monks by inviting them to big dinners at the church . . . and then, eventually, the monks themselves came to faith in Jesus.

"I think Cambodia can become a [largely] Christian nation within the next ten years," Ted says. (This hope is not without threats, for Muslim training facilities are also being built throughout the countryside. Though Cambodia's prime minister banned these in the wake of the September 11, 2001 terrorist attacks on the U.S., he recently re-opened the door to such activity. New Muslim centers are springing up across the country.)

In this time of great opportunity–and great spiritual conflict–a new generation of Christian believers is entering the arena. The children once rescued from the streets are now taking on leadership roles to rescue others.

For example, we met a girl I'll call Sy. Sy's mother died of AIDS when Sy was seven years old. She didn't know who her father was. She went to live in another village, with her grandmother. But by the time Sy was 13, her grandmother had become chronically ill and was no longer able to care for her.

Sy didn't know where to turn; she knew the dangers of the streets, with their pimps and brothels. But Sy did know how to pray, for she remembered her mother telling her about Jesus, that He was the only hope that would not fail, regardless of whatever else changed around her.

A pastor from the village came to Sy's grandmother's hut. He told her about the church that cares for children, and with the grandmother's blessing, brought Sy to the orphanage. She went to school. She learned more about Jesus. She grew to young womanhood in security, as part of a community of believers.

Sy wanted to pass on the blessings that had saved her. At age 20, she married a young Cambodian pastor . . . and today they are the houseparents for a new church-orphanage in Kompong Chhnang province. Above the cross in their sparkling, small sanctuary is a Scripture verse from Hebrews. It's the hope for Cambodia, the hope for any of us in today's changing world: *Jesus Christ is the same yesterday, today, and forever.*

About 30 years ago, it is said, a Chinese man discovered a small crack in his field. The earth had shifted during heavy rains, and a little crevasse had opened. Curious, the man probed it with a stick, and it opened into a hole. A deep hole. He called to his neighbors. They got ropes, climbed down into the widening fissure . . . and discovered an immense, extraordinary underground cavern full of astonishing stalactites, stalagmites, and intricate rock formations. Pearlized rocks formed delicate pillars; soaring, sparkling castles of rock reflected in still underground lakes. The wonders went on for miles.

Today people from all over the world come to visit these astounding caves. When I was with Dois visiting new churches in China recently, our hosts took us to explore them. As we walked down long underground pathways, marveling at the soaring, beautiful rock formations of this hidden world, I couldn't help but wonder: What if that Chinese man had ignored the small opening in his field? He could have said he was too busy to explore it, or too tired, or that it wasn't his business. He could have just covered it over and continued with his plan for the day.

But there was an amazing, unbelievable treasure just waiting to be discovered . . . and since the man paused, considered, and explored the unexpected thing in his path, the world is richer for it.

As I considered this, I couldn't help but be reminded of Dois's folksy statement about the way he looks for God's leading: "I just look under rocks."

In the midst of every commonplace day, God plants incredible opportunities in our path. The problem is that these aren't usually labeled with bright Post-it notes: *"Incredible opportunity here!" "Hidden treasure here!"*

No, most often these "chance" encounters just seem ordinary. But what I've seen in Dois is that if we are attuned to the urge of the Holy Spirit, actively seeking God's leading and His prompt in all things, He'll help us recognize His opportunities. And as we explore them, believing that God can do miracles, He'll start chains of events that can transform lives and communities forever.

Perhaps you've heard the story of the townspeople of a French village during World War II. After a terrible bombing, they wept when they saw the ruins of their cathedral. It had been the landmark of their town. Now it was rubble.

Yet the people sifted every shovel full of debris. They cleaned up the carnage. And deep within the piles of ash, they came upon the statue of Jesus that had once graced their cathedral's chancel.

The statue was mostly intact. Christ's arms were still extended as if He was tenderly calling the villagers to Himself. But with all that was spared, the hands had been destroyed. Christ's arms ended only in marble stubs.

The people thought sadly they must throw it away... until one wise person said this: "No. We must place the broken statue of Christ in our new cathedral. And we must put an inscription below Him that reads, *'He has no hands but our hands.'*"

There's no more appropriate way to close this book, for the story of the statue captures the contradiction of the God who hung on the cross, the God who limited Himself on this earth and chooses now to work through the likes of us. On His part, what could be more strange, or tender? On our part, what challenge could be more exhilarating? And yet how often we refuse it!

We're here on earth but a short while. Fresh winds are blowing, and the great road of faith runs like a ribbon before us. Opportunities are waiting on it. They may seem like interruptions or obstacles. Some may look like ordinary rocks. But in reality they are brilliant gems, "good works prepared in advance" by the God who continues, even in times of great challenge, to call people to Himself, all over the world.

And so the question, and the choice before us, is simply this: When we see God's opportunities on the road before us . . . will we pass them by? Or will we pick them up?

With Gratitude
Dois

To my wife, Shirley, daughters, Pam, Cindy, and Janice, as well as their husbands and children, who have supported, loved, and sacrificed for the ministry vision.

To Dick and Ginny Woodward, as they have continually led by their strong example of what a quadriplegic and an angel can do for the Kingdom.

To the POMOCO Group family, whose tireless efforts have provided a portion of the resources needed for continued ministry growth.

To the ICM Board, as they strive to keep us accountable, focused, and leveraged.

To the wonderful staff of ICM who have put up with me over all the years and give of their time, energy, and emotions for this high calling.

To Jim and Heather Gills, Caleb West, Ralph Doudera, and Frank Batten Jr., who have been great friends, partners, and supporters of the work at ICM. Without them, the ministry might not have been started and maintained.

To Dave Cauwels and Pat MacMillan, who have continually given their resources and counsel.

To Ellen Vaughn, whose efforts to clarify our thoughts and communicate God's work through this ministry have shaped this book.

To everyone who has partnered with us in this work, we are grateful for your help in furthering God's Kingdom through ICM.

With Gratitude
Ellen

I thank God for the rich pleasure of working on this book. I don't know of any other project I've done over the years that has so intrigued and expanded my faith. I'm so grateful for the solidarity of friends and family in the process. Thank you to the ICM family–staff, board, and supporters–and the extended Rosser family for your energetic help. Thank you to the extended Woodward family as well . . . what a gift to know you all! Emily, Haley, and Walker Vaughn, thank you for opening your hearts to children in faraway places. Thank you, Lee, for demonstrating Christ's selfless love to me. And last, a salute and thanks to Dois and Shirley Rosser, whose long, faithful walk with Christ has greatly encouraged my own journey with Him.

If
THE GOD WHO
HUNG ON THE CROSS
HAS BLESSED YOU...

Please help ICM bless believers around the world with
Mini Bible College and Church Buildings!

To be used for:

☐ Mini Bible College　　☐ Church Building

Enclosed is my first gift of:

☐ $50　　　　　☐ $100

☐ $200　　　　 ☐ $_____

Credit Card Information

Charge my card: ☐ one time　☐ monthly　☐ quarterly　☐ _____

☐ Visa　☐ Mastercard　☐ American Express　☐ Discover

Credit Card#: _____

3 Digit Security Code: _____ Expiration Date: _____

Name on Card (please print): _____

Signature: _____

Billing Address:

Street: _____ City: _____

State: _____ Zip: _____

Email Address: _____

For online giving, visit *www.icm.org/give*

Also available in audio
To order: Visit www.icm.org, mail in or call toll-free 1-877-622-7778

INTERNATIONAL COOPERATING MINISTRIES

The God Who Hung on the Cross
By Dois I. Rosser, Jr. and Ellen Vaughn

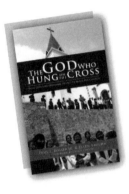

Suggested donation:

$13 - Paperback
$20 - 25th Anniversary Hardcover Edition
$18 - Audio

(Shipping and handling included)

To order more copies, call toll free
1.800.999.3892
or to order online, visit
www.icm.org

The 4 Spiritual Secrets
By Dick Woodward with Ellen Vaughn

Suggested donation: $13 Print | $18 Audio
(Shipping and handling included)

Visit Dick Woodward's blog site
at **www.4SpiritualSecrets.com**

Please specify delivery address.
We can ship to you or directly to friends and family.

Find out more about ICM and Mini Bible College products by visiting:
www.icm.org

I'd Like to Order More Copies

Shipping Information:

Name: _____

Address: _____

_____

Phone Number: _____

Email Address: _____

Quantity:

The God Who Hung on the Cross: ____Book *($13)* ____Audio *($18)*

____25*th* Anniversary Hardcover Edition *($20)*

The 4 Spiritual Secrets: _____ Book *($13)* _____ Audio *($18)*

Total: $_____ *(Above total includes shipping - 1-10 business days delivery)*
(Note: Goods and services have been received; no tax deductible amount)

Check Enclosed:__ *(Make check payable to ICM)*
Credit Card:__ *(Please enter information below)*

Credit Card Information:

Type: __ **Master Card** __ **Discover** __**Visa** __**Amercan Express***

Credit Card number: _____

Expiration Date: _____ Security Code: _____

Name on Card: _____

(Please print)

Billing Address: *(If different from the above address)*

_____

_____

* *If American Express, enter 4 digits in front for security code*

INTERNATIONAL COOPERATING MINISTRIES
606 Aberdeen Road, Hampton VA 23661
1-800-999-3892